BTOOOM!

JUNYA INOUE

07

THE COMPLETE CONQUER GUIDE

HIMIKO

GENDER: Female
AGE: 15
BLOOD TYPE: B
JOB: High school student
HOME: Tokyo
BIM TYPE: Timer

After Sakamoto defeated his first enemy player, Yoshiaki Imagawa, he ran across this mysterious high school girl. She harbors a deep resentment against men, but after surviving some battles thanks to Sakamoto, she begins to trust him and joins up with his team.

KIYOSHI TAIRA

GENDER: Male
AGE: 51
BLOOD TYPE: A
JOB: Real estate business manager
HOME: Osaka
BIM TYPE: Homing

Taira is a player Sakamoto came across while in pursuit of Himiko. He's a friendly man from the Kansai region who teams up with Sakamoto in hopes of getting off the island without resorting to murder. He is seriously injured by Miyamoto.

RYOUTA SAKAMOTO

GENDER: Male
AGE: 22
BLOOD TYPE: B
JOB: Unemployed
HOME: Tokyo
BIM TYPE: Timer

After spending every day cooped up in his home playing online, he suddenly wakes up to find that he's been taken to a mysterious deserted island and is being made to kill people just like in "BTOOOM!", the online third-person shooter he's really into.

IN ORDER TO ESCAPE WITH THEIR LIVES, THE THREE THEN START PUTTING THEIR HEADS TOGETHER TO UNRAVEL THE MYSTERIES OF THE ISLAND AND TO FLESH OUT THE CONSPIRACY THEORY ABOUT TYRANNOS JAPAN, THE DEVELOPER BEHIND "BTOOOM!", WHICH THEY BELIEVE HAS SOMETHING TO DO WITH THIS GAME OF DEATH. SOON SAKAMOTO AND HIMIKO COME ACROSS MASAHITO DATE, A DOCTOR. HAVING TREATED TAIRA'S WOUNDS, DATE WINS THE TRUST OF THE PAIR, BUT IN TRUTH, HE IS A REPEAT PLAYER OF THE GAME WHO SURVIVED SIX MONTHS EARLIER AND RETURNED HOME. SAKAMOTO AND HIMIKO ARE ALSO CONFRONTED BY THE MYSTERIOUS NOBUTAKA ODA, WITH HIS EXCEPTIONAL AGILITY AND CUNNING, AND HIDEMI KINOSHITA, WHO ISN'T AFRAID TO CHARGE INTO BATTLE. AND THEY'RE NOT ALONE! THE FAMILIAR FACE OF JUNIOR HIGH STUDENT KOUSUKE KIRA APPEARS ONCE MORE...! DEADLY "BTOOOM!" TAKES AN EXTREME TURN WITHIN THE DEPTHS OF THE ISLAND!

BTOOOM! OT

MASAHITO DATE

GENDER: Male
AGE: 40
BLOOD TYPE: AB
JOB: Doctor
HOME: Chiba
BIM TYPE: Remote Control

A survivor from an earlier game who collected all eight chips. He has a merciless, cruel personality and is particularly good at winning people over only to throw them under the bus. He's being made to play "BTOOOM!" over again.

SHIKI MURASAKI

GENDER: Female
AGE: 39
BLOOD TYPE: O
JOB: Nurse
HOME: Chiba
BIM TYPE: NO DATA

A mysterious woman Sakamoto and Himiko encountered while in the abandoned building. Since her left hand with the embedded chip has been severed, she doesn't appear on any radar. She's a player from the previous run of the game and was betrayed by her former colleague, Date.

KOUSUKE KIRA

GENDER: Male
AGE: 14
BLOOD TYPE: AB
JOB: Junior high student
HOME: Tokyo
BIM TYPE: Implosion

A student with a dark, brutal, murderous past, he has always been a big fan of "BTOOOM!". But now that it's come to life, he enjoys this game of "kill or be killed" even more, deep down. His dream is to defeat "SAKAMOTO," the top world ranker in "BTOOOM!".

NOBUTAKA ODA

GENDER: Male
AGE: 22
BLOOD TYPE: AB
JOB: Restaurant manager
HOME: Tokyo
BIM TYPE: Homing

A super-high-level player who has the ability to carry out elaborate plans with his superior athleticism. His all-or-nothing operations involve carefully laid traps to defeat his foes. He knows Sakamoto's past.

Story

OUR MAIN CHARACTER, RYOUTA SAKAMOTO, IS A TYPICAL NEET ("NOT IN EDUCATION, EMPLOYMENT, OR TRAINING") ONLINE GAMER. THEN ONE DAY, HE'S SUDDENLY KIDNAPPED BY MYSTERIOUS MEN IN BLACK AND TAKEN TO A DESERTED ISLAND. THERE, HE'S FORCED TO USE EXPLOSIVES CALLED BIMS IN A DEATH MATCH AGAINST PEOPLE LIKE HIM WHO HAVE ALSO BEEN BROUGHT TO THE ISLAND. IN FACT, THE WHOLE EXPERIENCE IS VIRTUALLY IDENTICAL TO THE GAME PLAY OF THE ONLINE THIRD-PERSON SHOOTER CALLED "BTOOOM!" THAT SAKAMOTO IS CURRENTLY INTO AND WITHIN WHICH HE RANKS AMONG THE WORLD'S BEST. IN THE GAME, PLAYERS USE A VARIETY OF EXPLOSIVES—INCLUDING TIMER, CRACKER, AND REMOTE TYPES—TO OBLITERATE THEIR OPPONENTS WITHOUT MERCY. NOW SAKAMOTO IS BEING FORCED TO PLAY THIS GAME IN REAL LIFE. WHILE FIGHTING TO STAY ALIVE, HE MEETS AND TEAMS UP WITH KIYOSHI TAIRA AND HIMIKO.

CONTENTS

CHAPTER 42 • OLD FRIEND 007

CHAPTER 43 • TRUE NATURE 053

CHAPTER 44 • PROVIDENCE 101

CHAPTER 45 • TWO SACRIFICES 147

FROM THE MOMENT WE'RE OLD ENOUGH TO UNDERSTAND WHAT'S GOING ON AROUND US, WE LEARN THE RULES OF SOCIETY.

WITH NO TIME TO THINK IT OVER, IT'S JUST DRILLED INTO US THAT THIS IS THE WAY THINGS ARE.
WHY...? HOW COME ...?

AND SOCIETY IS KEPT IN BALANCE,
AND SO, ORDER IS MAINTAINED.

...IT WAS THE SAME FOR ME...
OF COURSE...

MOST OF THEM END UP BEING TROUBLE.
BUT THERE ARE SOME PEOPLE WHO DEVIATE FROM THE USUAL ORDER.
THAT PERSON, FOR ME...
BUT ONCE EVERY SO OFTEN, ONE OF THEM PROVES TO BE AN EXCEP-TION.

42 Old Friend

NO MATTER WHERE I LOOK, I CAN'T FIND ANY CHIPS!!
NO!!

AFTER THAT CRAZY EXPLOSION HE SET OFF, THERE'S NO TELLING WHERE THEY FLEW OFF TO...

WHERE THE HELL'D THEY GO, DAMMIT !?

YOU'RE NOT RYOUTA, ARE YOU!?

WHOO.

...SOMETHING ABOUT HIM REMINDS ME OF ODA!
COME TO THINK OF IT...
...KNOW WHO I AM...?
HOW DOES THAT GUY...
SCREEN: UNLIMITED
GOAL!!
WHOO
WHOO
GOAL!!

JUST HOLD ON. ONE MORE GAME.
MY NEXT OPPO-NENT'S UP.
ARCADES ARE NO FUN WHEN YOU'RE ALL OUTTA CASH.
AREN'T YOU DONE YET?
WHOO-HOOOO!! THAT'S TEN WINS IN A ROW!!
PAN (SMACK)
...OR MORE LIKE...
HE WAS THE KINDA GUY WHO WAS JUST GOOD AT CON-TESTS.
...THE KINDA GUY WHO WAS PERFECT AT ANYTHING HE SET HIS MIND TO.

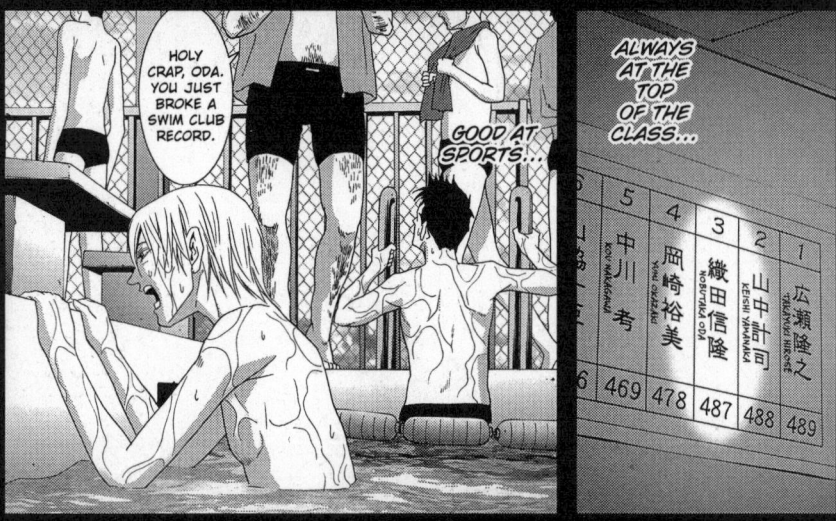
HOLY CRAP, ODA. YOU JUST BROKE A SWIM CLUB RECORD.
GOOD AT SPORTS...
ALWAYS AT THE TOP OF THE CLASS...
1 広瀬隆之 TAKAYUKI HIROSE 489
2 山中尚司 KEISHI YAMANAKA 488
3 織田信隆 NOBUTAKA ODA 487
4 岡崎裕美 YUMI OKAZAKI 478
5 中川考 KOU NAKAGAWA 469

NICE TO EVERYONE, A TON OF FRIENDS.

KYAH!
KYAH!
ODA-SENPAI!
SENPAI! ♡
YOU GUYS AREN'T EVEN ON THIS FLOOR!
AND A HIT WITH THE GIRLS, TO TOP IT ALL OFF...

I THOUGHT I WAS LIKE THAT TOO WHEN I WAS A KID, BUT...
WHATEVER HE DID, HE WAS A CUT ABOVE THE REST...
I DON'T KNOW IF HE COULD PICK UP ON THAT, BUT HE ALWAYS HUNG AROUND ME.
...I DIDN'T STAND A CHANCE NEXT TO HIM.
JUST BEING AROUND HIM GAVE ME AN INFERIORITY COMPLEX.
SO MAYBE IT WAS OUR SIMILAR SITUATIONS THAT ATTRACTED HIM TO ME.
HE DIDN'T LIVE WITH HIS DAD EITHER.

...MY TIME WITH ODA AT ALL...
THE REASON I ENJOYED...

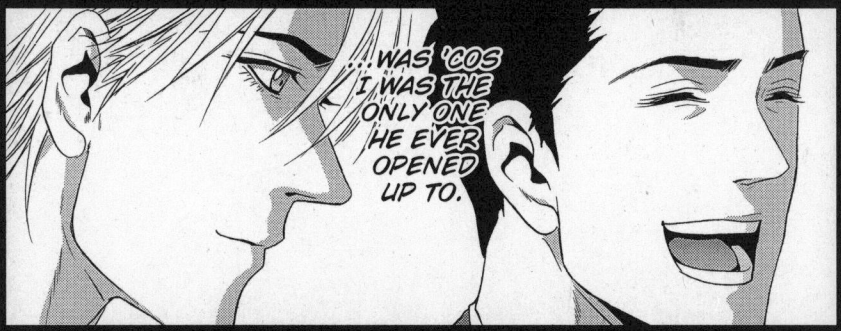
...WAS 'COS I WAS THE ONLY ONE HE EVER OPENED UP TO.

I HAD TO LIE ABOUT MY AGE.
KEEP IT DOWN, WOULD YA!?
Y'KNOW... I'VE ALWAYS HAD A MATURE FACE AND ALL...
FOR REAL ...!?
YOU STARTED WORKING PART-TIME AS A HOST?
I'LL BE FINE.
...ISN'T THAT A DAN-GEROUS LINE OF WORK?
WELL... SURE...
...I'LL STAY QUIET ABOUT IT, BUT...
YOU'RE SOME-THIN' ELSE...
I PRETTY MUCH RAKE IT IN JUST BY LISTENING TO TIRED OLD LADIES VENT.
IT'S ACTUALLY EASY MONEY, MAN!

I GOT NO CHOICE, DUDE.
THINGS ARE TIGHT AT HOME TOO.
BUT YOU KNOW WHAT ...
I'VE MADE UP MY MIND.
SOMEDAY I'LL RISE ABOVE ALL THIS ...
KASA (SHFF)
I'LL HAVE TO WORK AFTER I GRADUATE HIGH SCHOOL ANYWAY.
SO I MIGHT AS WELL START EARLY...
...AND GET MYSELF THAT TICKET OUTTA HERE...

GAAAA (SCARF)
...AND KEEP GOIN' STRAIGHT FOR MY DREAMS!
.....
..... AND WHAT DREAM IS THAT?
I WANNA BE A BILLION-AIRE!!

AND IT MADE ME REALLY HAPPY TO KNOW THAT AWE-INSPIRING ODA CONFIDED IN ME...
HE HAD THE ENERGY, THE INITIATIVE, AND THE HEAD FOR IT.
MOST PEOPLE WOULD LAUGH SOMEONE LIKE HIM IN THE FACE.
BUT, I FELT DEEP DOWN THAT HE COULD ACTUALLY DO IT.
...CONFIDED IN HIM TOO—
SO I...
JUICE BOX: BRILLIQUE
NOT SO LOUD!
RYOU-TA!!
YOU SERI-OUSLY GOT THE HOTS FOR AIKO!?

IF YOU LIKE HER, JUST TELL HER.
WHY NOT!?
SSH ...!! BE QUIET!
YOU IDIOT...!! I CAN'T DO THAT!
SO... YOU TELL HER YET?

SO WHY AREN'T YOU GONNA SAY ANY-THING?
AIKO SERI-ZAWA, HUH ...?
A LITTLE ON THE PLAIN SIDE, BUT STILL A BABE ...
I'M FINE WITH HOW IT IS NOW!!
I HAVE A RULE ABOUT NOT GOING BARGING INTO STUFF LIKE YOU.
FREAKIN' LAME...

THE WAY I SEE IT, RYOUTA ...
...YOU'RE TOTALLY NAIVE AND CONTENT TO HOLD YOURSELF BACK.
YOU'LL NEVER GET A SHOT AT GOING OUT WITH HER LIKE THAT.
YOU CAN ONLY SCORE IF YOU MAKE A MOVE, SEE?
THAT'S HOW THE WORLD WORKS ...

IF YOU STAY SO PASSIVE...
...ALL YOUR CHANCES WILL JUST KEEP GETTIN' AWAY FROM YOU.
THAT'S THE ONLY DIFFERENCE BETWEEN YOU AND ME.

JUST DROP IT...

AIKO ...?
WHAT'S WRONG ?
DID SOME-THING HAP-PEN!?
UWAAAAAAH!
I THOUGHT YOU WERE GOING OUT WITH ME!?
HEY, WHAT THE HELL, NOBU-TAKA!!?

DON'T YOU WALK AWAY FROM ME!!
NOBU-TAKA !!
SHUT UP.
WHAT IS IT? WHAT HAPPENED ...?
A LOVERS' SPAT...?
WHAT'S GOING ON?
HUH, ODA?

WELL...
...IT'S NOT SOME-THING I'M PROUD OF.
OKAY, SO...
...WHAT EXACTLY HAP-PENED?
I...
...SLEPT WITH AIKO.

AS FOR WHAT HE SAID AFTER THAT...
...I DIDN'T HEAR A WORD OF IT.
...WHAT EXCUSES HE MADE!...

SHE WASN'T EVEN THAT CLOSE A FRIEND.
...WASN'T MY GIRLFRIEND.
AS FAR AS I WAS CONCERNED, AIKO...

...HAD CRUSHED MY HEART, WHICH I'D OPENED UP EVER SO TIMIDLY TO HIM, UNDER HIS HEEL.
BUT I JUST FELT LIKE ODA...

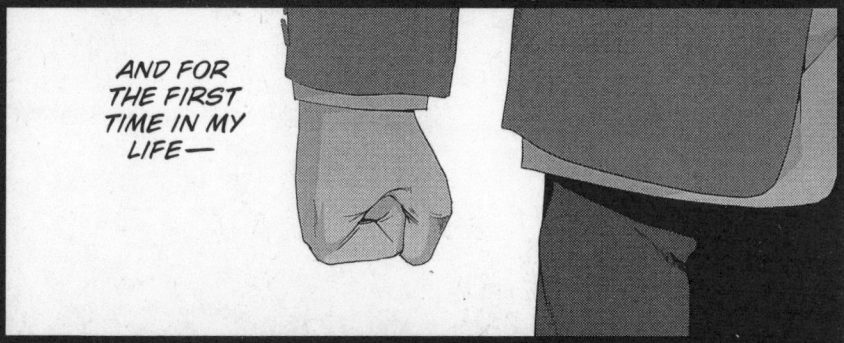
AND FOR THE FIRST TIME IN MY LIFE—

I PUNCHED SOMEONE.

...ABOUT WHERE AND HOW I'D LAND THE NEXT BLOW.
I WAS SURPRISINGLY CALM ABOUT THE WHOLE THING...
...AND I REMEMBER THINKING CAREFULLY...

BUT I MUST'VE BEEN SO WORKED UP THAT I COULDN'T HEAR WHAT WAS GOING ON AROUND ME...

...'COS BEFORE I KNEW IT, I WAS GETTING PULLED OFF OF HIM BY A CROWD OF PEOPLE.

HE NEVER CAME BACK TO SCHOOL AFTER THAT. HE JUST UP AND QUIT—
WE BOTH GOT SUSPENDED.
RUMOR HAD IT HE WENT ON WITH HIS CAREER AS A HOST...
...AND EVEN RAN A JOINT OF HIS OWN...
BUT I COULDN'T CARE LESS.
TAXI
...MAYBE I'D FEEL A LITTLE MORE CLOSURE ABOUT THE WHOLE THING...
IF I COULD JUST ASK HIM THAT...
BOOOM!
DADA!!
WHY'D HE GO AND DO A THING LIKE THAT ...?

THE WAY I SEE IT, RYOUTA...
...YOU'RE TOTALLY NAIVE AND CONTENT TO HOLD YOURSELF BACK.

WELL...
...I GUESS RYOUTA BEING HERE DOESN'T REALLY MATTER.

YOU!
YOU'RE NOT RYOUTA, ARE YOU!?

THAT REALLY WAS ODA.
I KNEW IT...
BTOOOM!
Soldiers, be ready!

IT'S NO WONDER HE PISSED SOMEONE OFF ENOUGH TO GET NOMINATED FOR THIS SHIT SHOW.
A GUY LIKE HIM...

BUT STILL...
...WILL HE BE MY ENEMY NOW...?

SFX: DOSU (WHUMP)

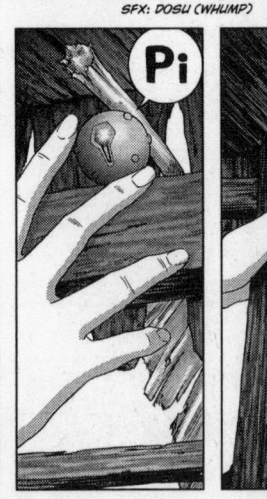

WE'LL CHILL OUT HERE, WHERE WE CAN KEEP AN EYE ON THINGS.
'KAY ...
IF THOSE GUYS FROM BEFORE TRACK US DOWN ...
... THEY'LL TRY THAT LITTLE HUT FIRST FOR SURE.
GOOD THINK-ING!
RYOUTA...

ZAAAA
ZAAAA (SSSHH)

?

PIKOOOON (PAAAAANG)

Soldiers, be ambitious!

GABA (JUMP)

BIIIIN
STIIIING
WAIT! HOLD ON!
IT'S ME! JUST ME!!
AN ENEMY !!

...THAT KID FROM BEFORE.

Y-YOU'RE ...

I HAVEN'T HAD A BITE TO EAT SINCE YOU LEFT ME BACK THERE ...
...SO I WAS HOPING... MAYBE YOU MIGHT SHARE SOME-THING...

THEN WHAT DO YOU WANT?

I DON'T HAVE BIMS ON ME ANY-MORE.
AND I DON'T WANNA FIGHT.
I MEAN IT.

FROM WHAT I JUST SAW, IT LOOKED LIKE YOU PICKED UP A CASE ...
DID YOU PUT IT SOME-WHERE?
WHERE IS IT?

HUH... SO YOU WERE JUST CRYING ABOUT THE CASE HERE...

AAAW ...
NO WAYYY ...!
DO (WHAP) !!

IT'S GONE ...
I DIDN'T GET IT.

?

THAT'S NOT IT.
I WANNA LEAVE, BUT I CAN'T.

IF IT MEANS NOT HAVING TO KILL PEOPLE, I'LL FIND EVERY LAST ONE, NO MATTER HOW LONG IT TAKES!
SHUT UP!
SO YOU'RE HOPING TO DIG UP THE CHIPS FROM THIS HUGE BEACH.
AH HA HA HA ...
FOR REAL!? THAT'S WHAT THIS IS ALL ABOUT !?
BUOOOO
!?
CHECK THIS OUT...
BUOO (VOOM)

BUOOO
WH—
WHAT IS THIS THING ...!?
BUOOO
A WAY TO LOOK FOR THE CHIPS.
YOU JUST PUT ENOUGH ENERGY INTO YOUR RADAR TO SEND OUT A CONSTANT WAVE.
THIS CAN PINPOINT THE CHIPS IN A RADIUS OF FIVE TO SEVEN METERS.
IT ALSO WORKS ON PLAYERS WHO'VE STOPPED MOVING AND ARE HIDING.
BUOO

BUOOO (VOOOOM)

BUOOO

ZAAAA (SSSSH)

OH YEAH. THIS CAME UP BEFORE TOO...
YOU DON'T REMEMBER?

LECTURE?

THAT'S WHY I'M THE ONLY ONE WITH HOLES IN MY MEMORY.

THAT HAD TO HAVE DONE IT!!
X360

!!
DO (THUD)

NIYA (SMIRK)

BUT I COULD BE SERIOUSLY SCREWED HERE—
AND HERE I THOUGHT I HAD THE ADVANTAGE, KNOWING "BTOOOM!" INSIDE OUT.

I BET YOU KNOW A WHOLE LOT MORE THAN YOU'RE LETTING ON, HUH?
SPILL IT!!
GA (GRAB)

IS THERE ANY-THING ELSE THEY TOLD US!?
ZA (ZSH)
ZA

HEY, KIRA !!
HUH ...?
WH-WHAT ...?

OVER-VIEW OF THE GAME ...?
YEAH ...

IF YOU PLAYED "BTOOOM!", IT'S STUFF YOU'D ALREADY KNOW.
BUT I GUESS MOST PEOPLE DIDN'T KNOW THE GAME, SO IT WAS PROLLY TOUGH FOR THEM TO UNDER-STAND.

THAN THE RADAR STUFF, IT WAS JUST THE DIFFERENT BIMS AND AN OVERVIEW OF THE GAME...
THEY ONLY HAD ABOUT ONE OR TWO MINUTES FOR IT.

...ODA HAS TO KNOW THIS TECHNIQUE TOO...
WAIT...
THIS MEANS...
...HE'S ALREADY GATHERED UP ALL HIS CHIPS.
IN WHICH CASE...
ZAAA (SSSHH)
WE CAN'T STAY HE—
ZAAA

!!
A BIM POUCH ...?
WHAT ...?
HUH ...?
CRAP ...

I DID IT!!
BIMS!!
THAT WAS SO EASY ...
... BACK IN THE GAME!
NOW I'M...

WHEN DID I LET GO OF IT!?
IT WAS HEAVY AND CLUNKY, SO I HAD THAT ONE IN MY HAND...

AH! THAT LITTLE ...
HE HAS MY BIMS !?

WAS THAT WHAT HE WAS AFTER FROM THE START? THAT'S WHY HE COZIED UP TO ME?

DON'T YOU SCREW WITH ME!!

EEP ...!

DA (DASH)

...
...

ZAAAA
(SSSHHH)

ZA

ZAZAA

IT'S STILL FRESH ...

...THE ENEMY'S PROB-ABLY CLOSE TOO.

SAKA-MOTO-KUN MUST BE NEARBY ...
THAT SAID...

BTOOOM!-43

43 TRUE NATURE

TA
TA
TA
TA
TA
TA
TA (STMP)
TA
QUIT SCREWING AROUND ...
...AND GIVE ME BACK THOSE BIMS!!
IN YOUR DREAMS !!
THESE BIMS ARE MINE!
AND I'M BACK IN THE GAME AGAIN!!

WHERE ARE YOU !!?
GET YOUR BUTT OUT HERE, KIRAAA!!

BUON (WHOOM)
KA (FLASH)
BUUUUUUUN (VOOOOOOM)
BE A GOOD KID AND C'MON OUT!!
YOU'RE CLOSE ENOUGH TO HEAR ME, AREN'T YOU?
IT'S NO USE TRYING TO HIDE!!
BUOOO

HFF!
ハア
HFF!
ハア
KAPA (POP)
カパッ
OR ELSE...
...I'LL KILL YOU, GOT IT ...?
EH HEH HEH ...
HURRY UP AND GO AWAY !!
JUST GET LOST!

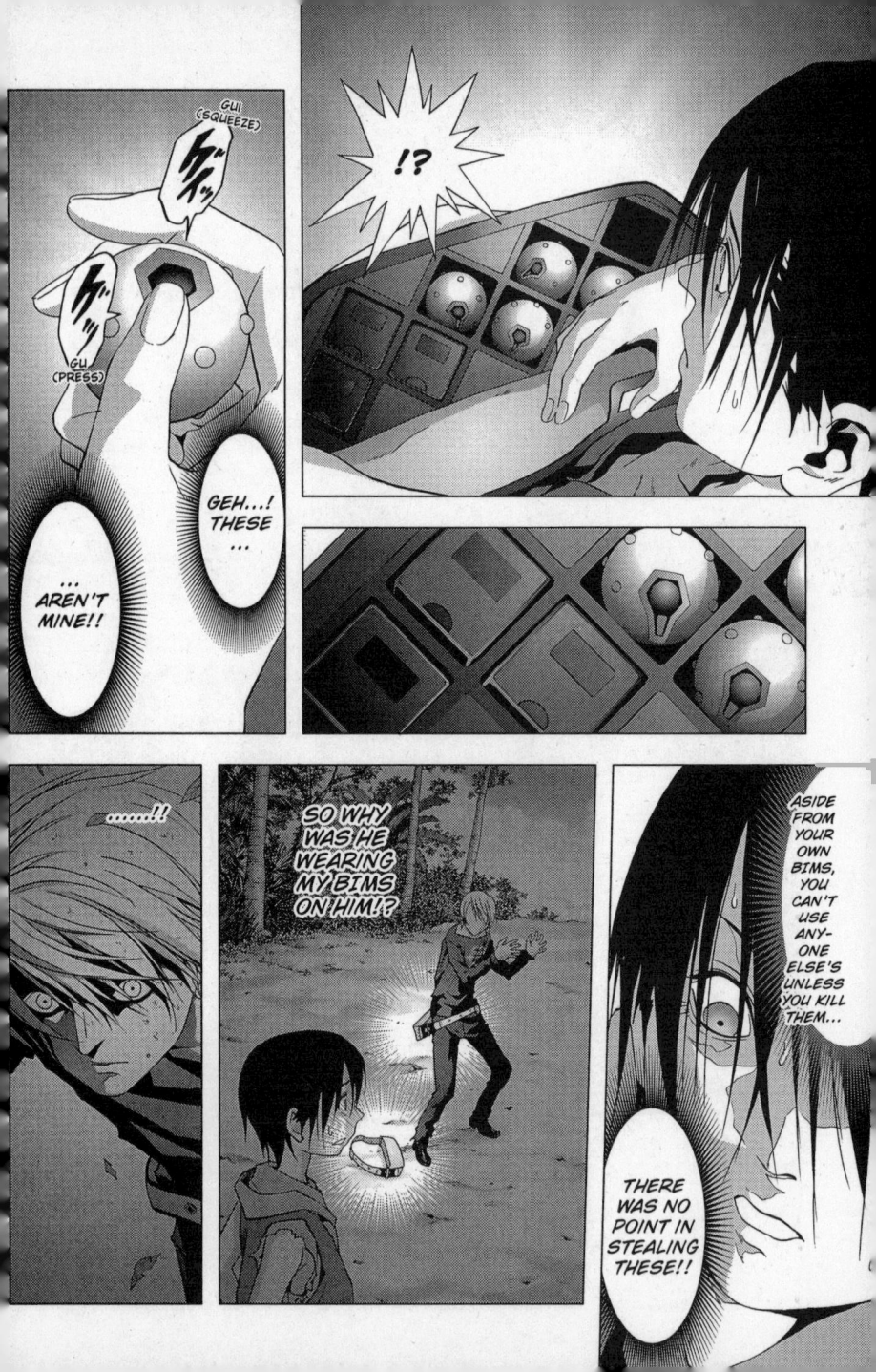
GUI (SQUEEZE)
GU (PRESS)
GEH...! THESE ...
... AREN'T MINE!!
!?
.....!!
SO WHY WAS HE WEARING MY BIMS ON HIM!?
ASIDE FROM YOUR OWN BIMS, YOU CAN'T USE ANY-ONE ELSE'S UNLESS YOU KILL THEM...
THERE WAS NO POINT IN STEALING THESE!!

...AND DROPPED THE POUCH AT HIS FEET ON PURPOSE TO TEST ME...?
DON'T TELL ME HE KNEW I WAS GONNA STEAL THE BIMS...
THERE YOU AAARE !!
IS THAT IT?
HE'S TAKING HIS SWEET TIME LOOKING FOR ME 'COS HE KNOWS I CAN'T ATTACK ...?
THAT'S THE WORLD RANKER SAKA-MOTO FOR YOU...

GA (WHOMP)
WAH!!
GUH!!

DOSUN (THUD)
BAKI
BAKI (SNAP)
GASASA (RUSTLE)
AAAAAAAH!!
OW, OW, OW ...
NGH ...!
YOU LITTLE SHIT, I OUGHTA BE ASKING Y—
THE HELL D'YOU THINK YOU'RE DOING ...!?

THIS HAS TO BE A BAD JOKE ...
WHAT THE HELL ARE WE S'POSED TO DO NOW!? HEY!!

ZAZAA (SSSHH)
ア

AND SAKA-MOTO-KUN'S STILL IN HIDING.
SO THAT ...

ONE DEAD BODY ...
...WITH ITS BIMS AND CHIPS SCAV-ENGED.

...TELLS US HE'S IN THE MIDDLE OF A FIGHT.

NO!!
DON'T USE YOUR RADAR CARE-LESSLY !!

THEN WE HAVE TO FIND HIM FAST ...

UNTIL JUST A WHILE AGO, WE WERE PICKING UP THE SIGNALS OF SEVERAL PEOPLE.
SAKA-MOTO-KUN ISN'T NECES-SARILY UP AGAINST THE GUY IN THE SHADES.
IF WE MINDLESSLY GIVE AWAY OUR POSITIONS, WE'LL BE KILLED...

THEN ...
...WHAT SHOULD WE DO?

WE'LL SET A TRAP.
KAPA (POP)
RADARS COME AFTER.

DON'T FORGET! THE MOST IMPORTANT THING IS YOUR OWN LIFE...
IF YOU'RE NOT CAREFUL, YOU'LL BE BUYING A TICKET STRAIGHT TO HELL.

WHAT THE HECK ~?
DIDN'T YOU MEAN TO LET 'EM GET STOLEN TO TEST ME?
THIS IS ALL YOUR FAULT, STEALING SOME-BODY ELSE'S BIMS!!
LOOK WHAT YOU'VE DONE!
I NEVER TRUSTED YOU FROM THE VERY START!
WHAAAAAT !!?
WHO THE HELL WOULD DO A DUMB-ASS THING LIKE THAT!!?
I LUCKED OUT WHEN YOU STOLE THIS ONE ...
JUST BY CHANCE ...
THEN WHY'D YOU HAVE MY POUCH ON YOU?

A GUY LIKE THIS AT THE TOP OF THE WORLD RANKINGS...
WHAT A LET-DOWN...
.....
BUT IT'S THANKS TO THEIR CUSHION THAT WE DIDN'T GET SERIOUSLY HURT.
THERE'S SO MANY BROKEN BRANCHES AND DEAD LEAVES, IT'S HARD TO TELL.
WHAT IS THIS PLACE ANYWAY? SOME KIND OF WATER TANK?
I SQUISHED IT JUST IN CASE.
O-OHH... THANKS.
CARE-FUL.
I SAW A CENTIPEDE CRAWLING AROUND THERE A SECOND AGO.
WHA—!?
DON'T ASK ME. HOW SHOULD I KNOW?

OUR MAIN PROBLEM IS FINDING A WAY OUTTA HERE...
YEAH ...
CAN YOU REACH THE RIM IF YOU JUMP?
LEMME TRY...
ZURU (SLIP)
WAAAH!
GWAH!!
DOSA (WHUMP)

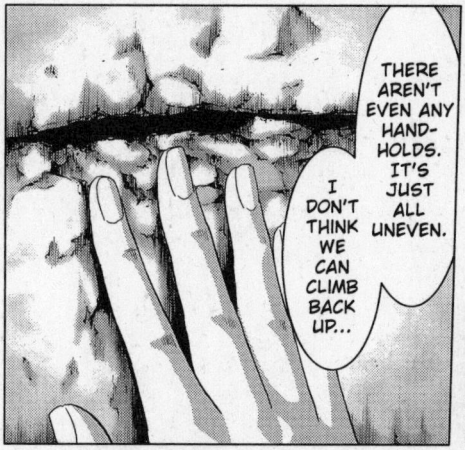
THERE AREN'T EVEN ANY HAND-HOLDS. IT'S JUST ALL UNEVEN.
I DON'T THINK WE CAN CLIMB BACK UP...

DAMN...
THE WALLS ARE PRETTY SLICK ...

IT'S DOWN TO US.
LEND ME YOUR SHOUL-DERS, KIRA.

WELL...
PAN
PAN (PAT)

NEITHER ONE OF US IS GETTING OUT OF THIS IF WE DON'T WORK TO-GETHER.

STAND UP AND GIMME A BOOST!!
I'M NO-WHERE NEAR CLOSE ENOUGH !!
HNGH!
GUUUUUH...
EASY ...
... FOR YOU ... ... TO SAY ...
GWAAH!!
DOSA (THUD)
WHOA!
DOSA

YOU GOT IT ALL MIXED UP!!
ANYWAY, ISN'T THE LIGHTER PERSON S'POSED TO GO ON TOP?

ONCE YOU GOT TO THE TOP, YOU'D RUN AND LEAVE ME HERE TO ROT!!
I CAN'T TRUST YOU.

YOU'RE PUSHING IT! I'M JUST A SCRAWNY JUNIOR HIGH KID WHO SPENDS ALL HIS TIME ONLINE.
HOLD ME UP BETTER NEXT TIME!

THIS IS STILL ALL YOUR FAULT.
OH, SHUT UP!
WHAT-EVER... YOU WON'T TRUST ME BUT WANT MY HELP? PLEASE!

IF ONLY I COULDA HAD SOMETHING TO EAT...
GUUU (GRRROWL)
ぐぅ〜
.....

HELP ME OUT, AND YOU CAN COME TOO.
WHAAA —!? SAKA-MOCCHAN, YOU'RE PLANNING TO HIJACK A HELI-COPTER?
IF I WAS IN CHARGE, I'D TURN OFF THE BIM DETONATION SWITCHES WHEN THE CHOPPERS GOT CLOSE.
WE'RE DEALING WITH PEOPLE WHO CREATED THIS LARGE-SCALE GAME SYSTEM, REMEM-BER?
...NO WAY.

BUT SOME OF THE PLAYERS HAVE KNIVES AND STUN GUNS ON THEM.
IF WE WORKED TOGETHER, I'M SURE WE'D STAND A CHANCE.
I SEE ...

I'M NOT SAYING I DO.
HOW DO YOU KNOW THEY WOULDN'T COME AT YOU WITH MACHINE GUNS BLAZING ...?

...THERE'S JUST SOMETHING ABOUT ALL THIS THAT FEELS OLD AND ANALOG, NOT SYSTEMATIC.

CALL IT A GAMER'S, OR MORE LIKE A DEBUGGER'S, HUNCH, BUT...
WHAT'S THAT ...?

I'M SURE THAT THE BALANCE IS THROWN OFF WHEN SOMEONE GETS OUT OF THE GAME...

I FOUND MORE BLIND SPOTS IN THE "BTOOOM!" SYSTEM THAN ANY OTHER DEBUGGER.
I GOT IT THAT MUCH CLOSER TO PERFECT.
I CAN PRACTICALLY SMELL OUT THE HOLES IN A SYSTEM...

HOW IS IT EVEN FAIR FOR ONE OF TYRANNOS'S DEBUGGERS TO BECOME A WORLD RANKER?
THAT'S FOUL PLAY IN THE EYES OF A REGULAR GAMER LIKE ME.
...YEAH, WELL—
WAIT A SECOND!! DON'T TRY TO CHANGE THE SUBJECT!!
BUT —!

LOOK... I'M NOT WITH YOU ON THAT LITTLE PLAN OF YOURS, BUT...

LET'S HEAR IT.
IF YOU'RE GONNA SAY YOU GO UP FIRST, YOU CAN FORGET IT.
...AS FAR AS GETTING OUT OF HERE, WHY DON'T WE TRY MY IDEA?
IT'S AN EVEN BETTER IDEA.
?
NOPE! I'M NOT SURE I COULD EVEN PULL YOU UP WHEN I GOT TO THE TOP, MOCCHAN.

WE'LL BLOW A WAY OUT USING ONE OF MY IMPLOSION BIMS!
BUT I'M THE ONLY ONE WHO CAN DETONATE THEM.
SO I WANT YOU TO TRUST ME.
I'D BE STUPID TO GO ON THE ATTACK IN A TIGHT PLACE LIKE THIS, RIGHT?
YOU GOT IT! ♡
BUT IF YOU TRY ANYTHING FUNNY AGAIN...
... CONSIDER YOURSELF DEAD.
FINE...

THERE'S ONLY SO MANY PLACES ONE CAN WALK IN A FOREST.
SO IF WE JUST FOCUS OUR TRAPS ON THESE AREAS, WE'LL HAVE THE UPPER HAND.
IT'S NO DIFFERENT FROM THE HALLWAYS IN A SCHOOL.
IN AN UN-TOUCHED FOREST LIKE THIS, IT'S VERY HARD TO WALK ANY-WHERE BUT THESE ANIMAL TRAILS ...
...IS DEFI-NITELY OFF...
YUP, THIS GUY...

DATE-SAN!!
HOW IS IT YOU KNOW ALL THIS STUFF?

DIDN'T YOU SAY WE WERE THE FIRST PEOPLE YOU'D MET IN THE FOUR DAYS SINCE COMING TO THIS ISLAND?

YOU'VE NEVER USED YOUR BIMS ...
...AND YOU'RE A DOC-TOR...
...SO HOW COME YOU KNOW ABOUT SETTING TRAPS WITH BIMS !!?

I DON'T GET IT.
Y—
YOU ...

AND BACK THERE ...
...YOU TRIED TO KILL ME WITH THAT BIM TOO, DIDN'T YOU?

YOU'VE BEEN LYING TO US!!
.....

IS SOME-THING THE MATTER, HIMIKO-KUN?
IF I DID, I'D BE PUTTING MYSELF IN DANGER.
I CAN'T SAY THAT ...!!
OH NO... I WAS JUST THINKING YOU'RE AMAZING FOR COMING UP WITH THIS...
IT'S A REAL RELIEF ...

IT'S NO BIG DEAL...

IF I STAY WITH HIM ANY LONGER, I'LL...
RYOUTA...
...WHERE ARE YOU ...?

...COME BACK SOON ...!!
PLEASE...

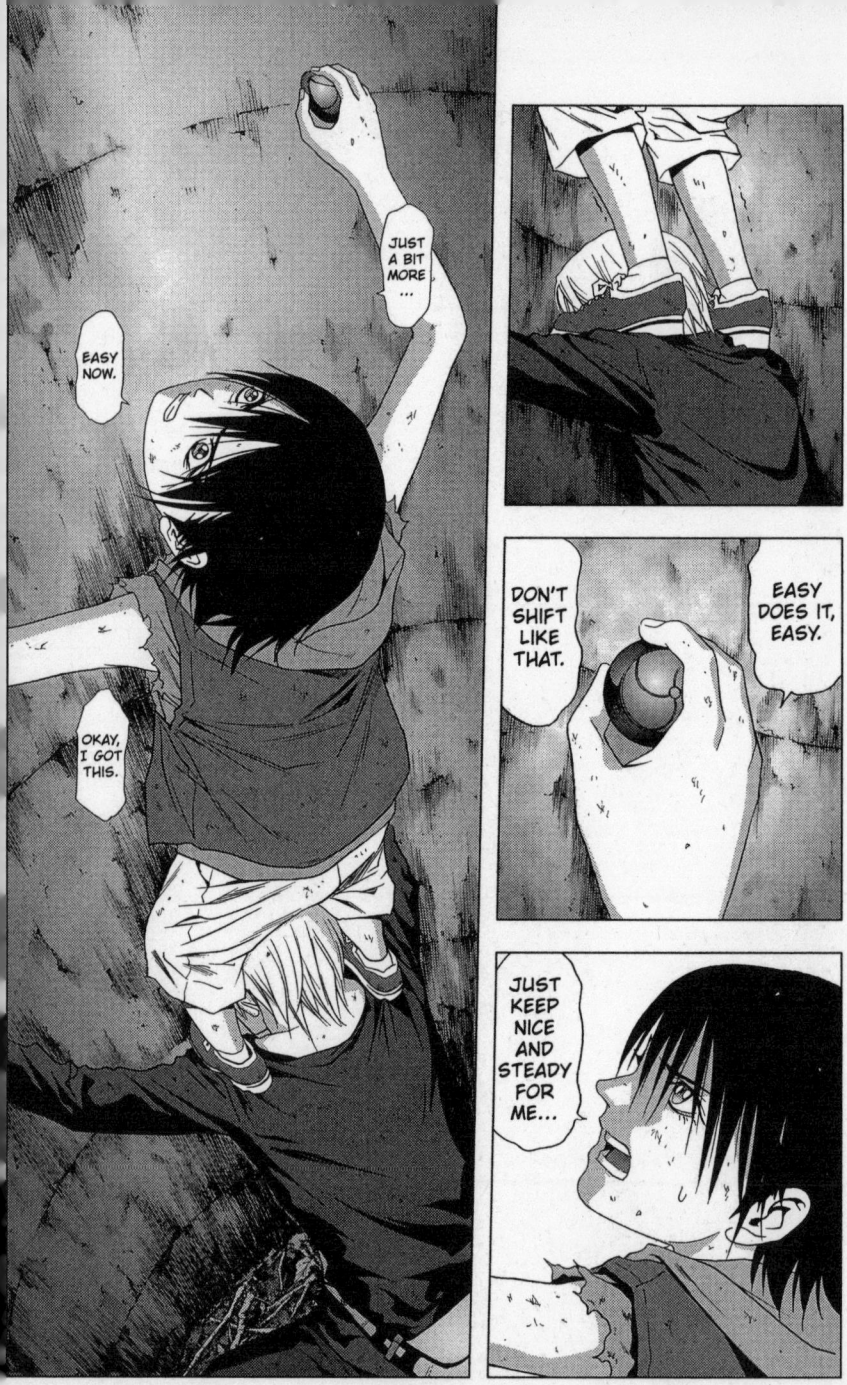
JUST A BIT MORE ...
EASY NOW.
OKAY, I GOT THIS.
EASY DOES IT, EASY.
DON'T SHIFT LIKE THAT.
JUST KEEP NICE AND STEADY FOR ME...

I WANNA MAKE IT EASIER FOR US TO REACH THE NEXT STEP UP.
SO I HAVE TO SET IT AS HIGH AS POSSIBLE...

ARE YOU DONE YET ...?
THIS SHOULD BE GOOD ENOUGH ...

KAN (KONK)
BTOOOM!

MAKE SURE YOU SET IT GOOD AND TIGHT.
WHATEVER YOU DO, DON'T DROP IT...

SHAKON (SHNK)
UGH ...!
GA (CLAN)
KUH ...!
GA
GA
OOF!!
DAN (THUMP)

YOU TRUST PEOPLE TOO MUCH!
DUMB ASS!!
SHUGOOO (WHOOOOOSH)

YOU GOTTA BE KIDDING ME!?
SHUGOOOOOOOO (SHWOOOOOP)
...WHERE IS THE DAMN THING...!?
GOO (WHOOSH)
BUT...
I GOTTA TURN OFF THE SWITCH.
GOOO (WHOOSH)

THIS IS THE END OF THE ROAD FOR HIM.
...SOME BIMS CAN'T BE DEACTI-VATED...
DON'T TELL ME...
I WIN!!
CA (STOMP)
DON'T UNDER-ESTIMATE ME!!
D—

NO WAY ...!?
HUH ...?
ZAZAZA (SCRRRTCH)
GASHI (GRAB)
DOSA (WHUMP)
AAH!!

SHUGOOO (SHWOOP)
STOP THIS THING RIGHT NOW, KIRA !!
I DON'T KNOW HOW!!
DON'T ASK ME!! YOU WERE THE ONLY ONE S'POSED TO DIE!!
THEN WHAT THE HELL DO WE DO, YOU DAMN BRAT !!?
GA (WHOK)
DON'T FUCK WITH ME!!

GO
(VOOM)

KAN
(CLACK)
KON
(KONK)

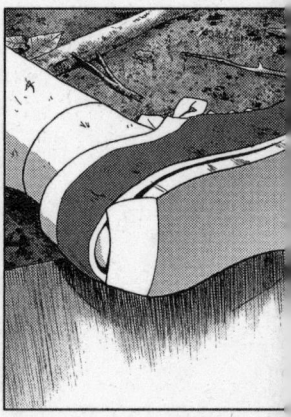

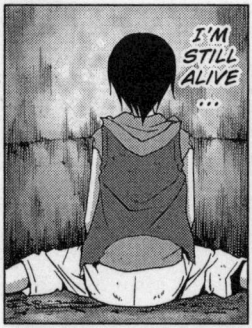
I'M STILL ALIVE ...

I...

PICHAN (PLOSH)
CHAPUN (SPLISH)

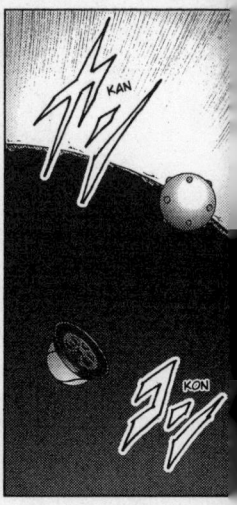
KAN
KON

A HOLE ...?
BA (HOP)
BA'SHA (SPLASH)
WAIT... WHAT'S HE UP TO?
BASHA

A DRAIN ...?
BTOOOM!

I'M TAKING THESE BIMS WITH ME, 'KAY ~!?
BYE-BYYYE!

A-HA! ♡ WORKS FOR ME!

...I DON'T EVEN FEEL LIKE DOING ANY-THING ABOUT IT NOW...
BTOOOM!

THEY MUST'VE FALLEN OUT THROUGH THERE...
THIS POUCH HAS HOLLOWS IN IT...

BUT...

THIS TIME THEY ACTUALLY WERE HIS BIMS...
NOT GOOD...

—RIGHT AFTER THAT, I FELT HIMIKO'S DOUBLE ECHO...
...AND DATE-SAN HELPED ME OUT.
THANKS, HIMIKO...
THANK YOU, DATE-SAN.

H-
HIMIKO
...

SU (SWF)

FOUR DAYS SINCE THE START OF THE GAME, 1:30 PM—
I DIDN'T GET ANY FOOD AND HAD BIMS STOLEN FROM ME, BUT...
...I WAS STILL ALIVE ...

ER... LOOK... I...
...HAVEN'T BATHED IN A WHILE, SO...
S-SORRY ...
NO, I'M SORRY ...

BTOOOM!

BTOOOM!

BTOOOM!

09

08

BTOOOM!

BTOOOM!

07

06

BTOOOM!

05

04

03

BTOOOM!

02

BTOOOM!

01

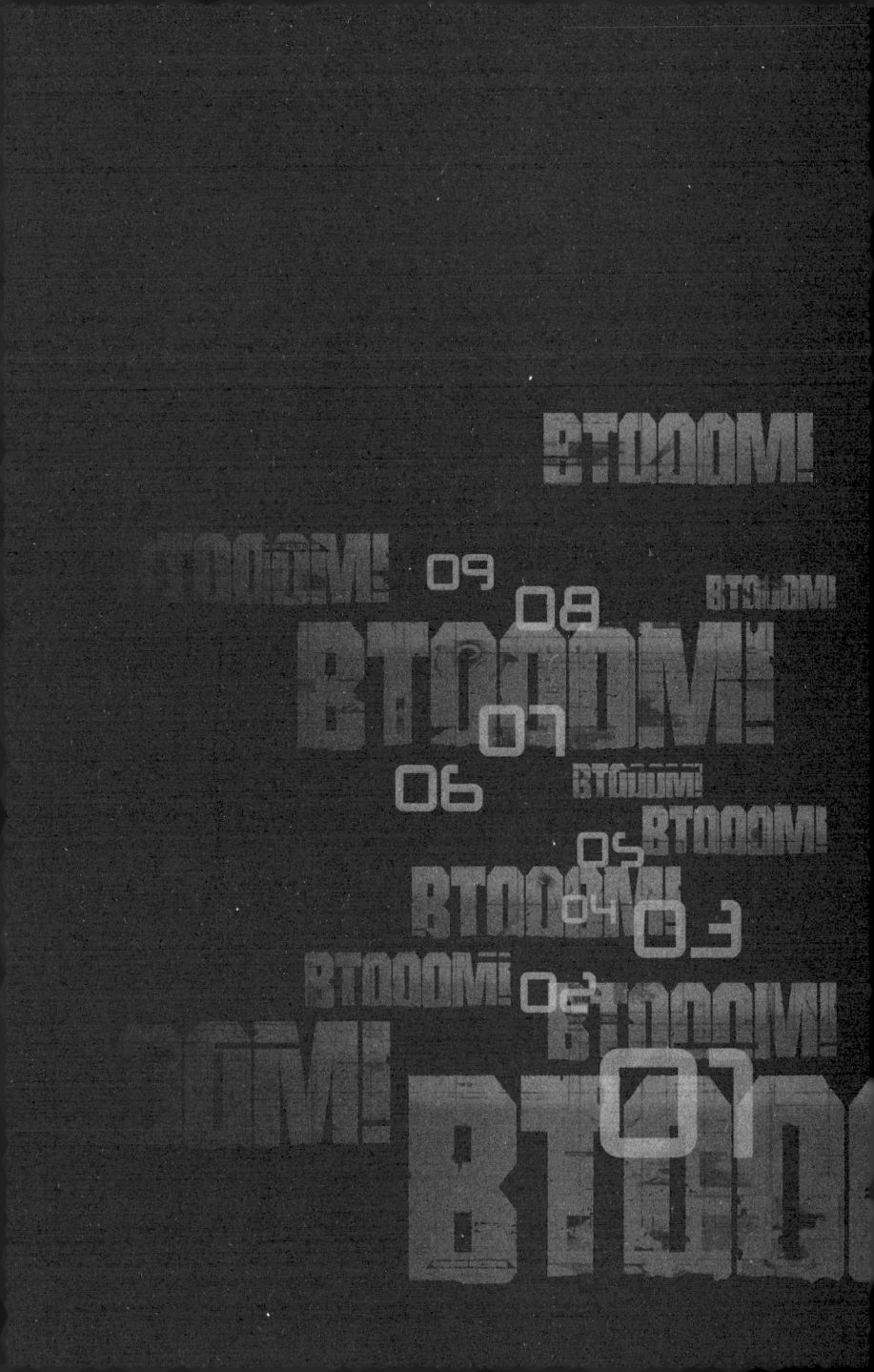
BTOOOM!
09
08
07
06
05
04
03
02
01

44 PROVIDENCE

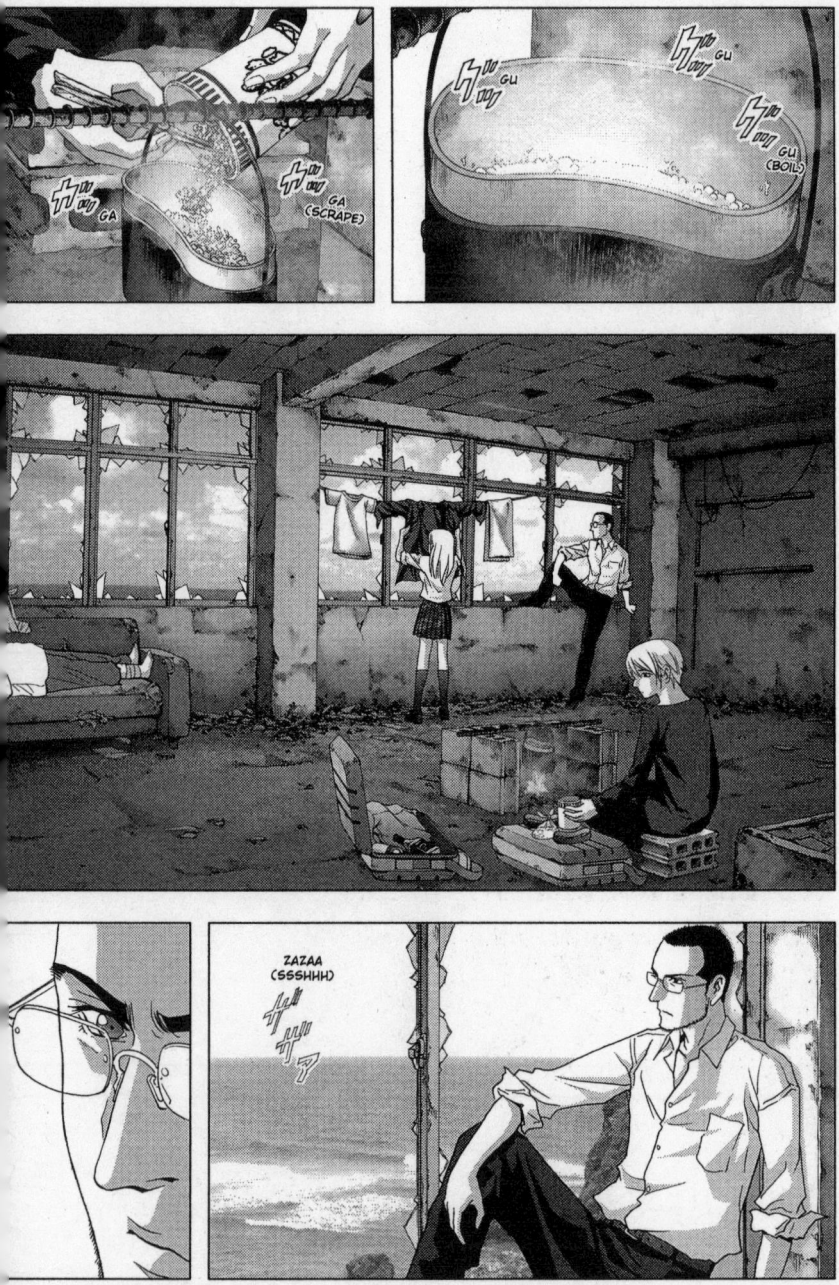
GA
GA (SCRAPE)
GU
GU
GU (BOILS)
ZAZAA (SSSHHH)

AND AS IF THAT WASN'T SHITTY ENOUGH, NOW I'M STUCK SHARING WHAT LITTLE FOOD I HAD LEFT...

IN THE END, WE DIDN'T GET ANY FOOD AND HAD TO RUN BACK WITH OUR TAILS BETWEEN OUR LEGS.
KEH...! BAS-TARDS!

THERE'S ONLY ALCOHOL AND RICE LEFT, BUT IT SHOULD FEED US FOR AT LEAST ONE DAY.
SURE... I LUCKED OUT AND GOT IT THE FIRST DAY...

I CAN'T BELIEVE YOU HAD A CASE TOO, DATE-SAN.
MAN, WHAT A REAL GOD-SEND!

WE REALLY APPRE-CIATE IT.
AND IT EVEN HAD RICE ...

CAN'T HAVE THEM WON-DERING HOW I KNOW SO MUCH ...
CRAP ...

HUH...? ANOTHER PLANE'S COMING TOMOR-ROW TOO?
LET'S TRY TO GET SOME MORE TO-MOR-ROW.

SINCE GETTING THIS CASE ON THAT FIRST... DAY...
...I HAVEN'T BEEN ABLE TO STOP THINKING ABOUT GETTING MORE FOOD, COWARD THAT I AM.
...I DON'T THINK IT'D BE WRONG TO ASSUME THEY'LL BE BACK TOMOR-ROW, YOU KNOW?
EVERY DAY AROUND MIDDAY, I'VE BEEN HEARING THE ENGINES, SO...
CUP: GIN-CHAN NOODLES
NOW... DINNER IS SERVED!!
THAT'S AMAZ-ING!
HERE WE GO.
KNOWING THAT, WE'RE SURE TO GET THE FOOD BEFORE ANYBODY ELSE!!
CURRY NOODLE POR-RIDGE!
SMELLS GREAT...
SINCE THERE WAS SO LITTLE, I REALLY SOAKED THEM TO MAKE MORE.
IT'S A LITTLE BLAND, BUT I'M SURE IT'LL HIT THE SPOT.

HERE, TAIRA-SAN.
EAT UP.

THAT WON'T DO, TAIRA-SAN!!
...DON'T FEEL... LIKE EATING ...

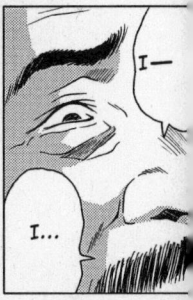
I—
I...

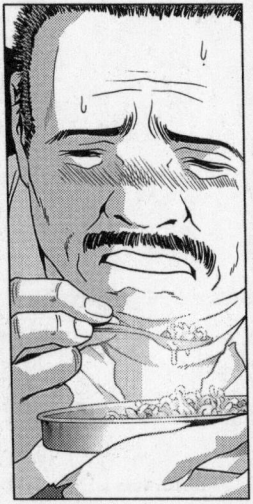

IF YOU DON'T REGAIN YOUR STRENGTH, YOU'LL NEVER GET BETTER.
HERE ...

MIND IF I TAKE A LOOK AT HIM?
DATE-SAN.

TAIRA-SAN!!
KOKLIN (CLATTER)
コクリン
BESHA (SPLAT)
ベシャッ

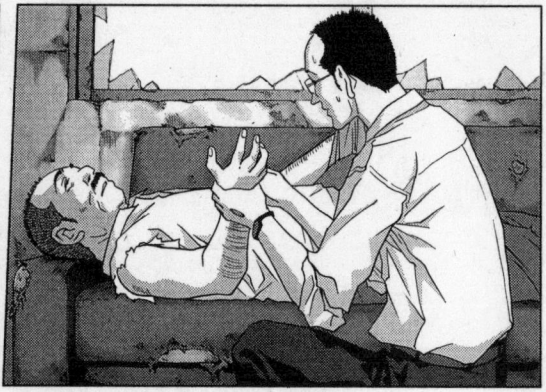

BTOOOM!

BECAUSE OF THE POISON FROM THE LIZARD'S BITE...
...HIS WOUND WON'T STOP BLEEDING AT ALL...

THIS IS BAD ...

THE BITE OF THE KOMODO IS DEFINITELY VENOMOUS.
THAT'S AN OUT-DATED THEORY.

BUT ON TV THEY SAID THAT KOMODO DRAGONS AREN'T POISON-OUS...
POI-SON ...?

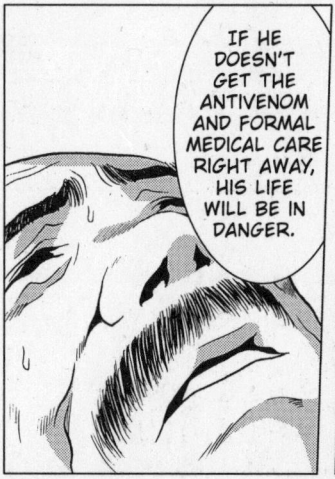
IF HE DOESN'T GET THE ANTIVENOM AND FORMAL MEDICAL CARE RIGHT AWAY, HIS LIFE WILL BE IN DANGER.

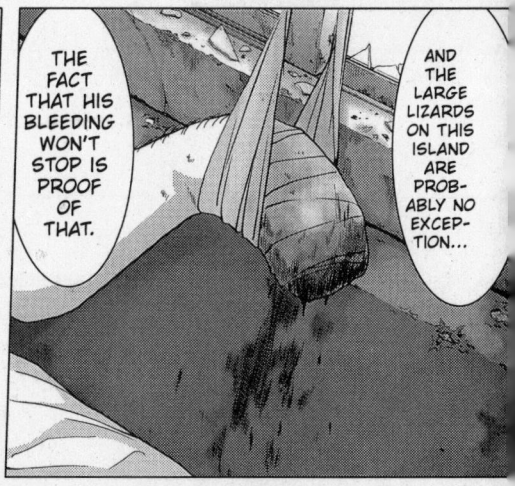
THE FACT THAT HIS BLEEDING WON'T STOP IS PROOF OF THAT.
AND THE LARGE LIZARDS ON THIS ISLAND ARE PROB-ABLY NO EXCEP-TION...

N-NO.
THAT CAN'T BE...
BTOOOM!
CAN WE TALK ...?
RYOU-TA...
MURA-SAKI-SAN SAID THERE WAS A MEDICAL STORE-ROOM.
I'M SURE SOME-THING THERE WILL HELP.
SHH!
YOU WANNA GO BACK TO THOSE RUINS ...?

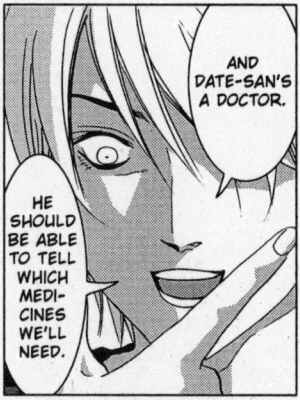
AND DATE-SAN'S A DOCTOR.
HE SHOULD BE ABLE TO TELL WHICH MEDICINES WE'LL NEED.

RIGHT... SO IF THE PEOPLE WHO USED THAT BUILDING BEFORE PREPARED FOR ANY KIND OF LIZARD ATTACK...
...IT WOULDN'T BE OUT OF THE QUESTION FOR THEM TO HAVE AN ANTIDOTE OR SOMETHING!

YOU WANT HIM TO COME TOO?
YEAH. WHY NOT ...?

EH ...?
DATE-SAN ...?

I THINK IT MAKES TOTAL SENSE TO BRING DATE-SAN SINCE HE'S BEEN TREATING TAIRA-SAN.
WAIIIT, BUT —!

CAN'T WE JUST HAVE MURA-SAKI-SAN PICK OUT WHAT WE'LL NEED ...?

HERE YOU ARE.
I RINSED OFF ALL THE DIRT.
THANKS...
CHORORO (GUUUUSH)
ズズ!
ZUZU (SLURP)
ジュル!
JURU (SHLORP)
SHIT ...!
I CAN'T BELIEVE WE'RE WASTING PRECIOUS FOOD ON THIS GUY WHO'S AS GOOD AS DEAD...

THE TIME HAS ARRIVED...

I'M NOT GETTING ANYTHING OUT OF TEAMING UP WITH THESE GUYS ANY-MORE.

...HOW SHOULD I SET MY TRAP?
ONLY QUESTION IS...

SURE... I DON'T MIND.
THERE MIGHT BE AN ANTIDOTE OR SOMETHING ELSE TO HELP TAIRA-SAN.
THEY HAVE A MEDICAL STORE-ROOM THERE.
WOULD YOU COME WITH US ...?
HUH...? RUINS?

WHAT WAS THAT FOR !!?
OWW!
GYUU (PINCH)

IT'S A LITTLE BULKY, BUT...
... LET'S TAKE THIS WITH US.
WE MIGHT NEED SOMETHING TO PUT IT ALL IN, SO...

WELL, TAIRA-SAN... OFF WE GO.
WE'LL BE BACK QUICK, OKAY?

.....

I...CAN'T TRUST HIM AT ALL.
DO YOU HAVE SOMETHING AGAINST DATE-SAN?
HEY, HIMIKO ...
...WHEN I WAS WRESTLING WITH THAT GIRL...
SEE, BEFORE ...
FOR REAL ?
SEEMS LIKE TOO NICE A GUY TO MERIT ENOUGH HATE TO GET SENT TO THE ISLAND, IF YOU ASK ME.

Pi

...HE THREW A BIM AIMED TO TAKE US BOTH OUT.

I HAVE NO REASON TO TRUST THAT GUY.
YET HE TRIED TO SMOOTH OVER IT AND ACTED LIKE HE'D SAVED ME.

I ONLY JUST MANAGED TO PROTECT MYSELF FROM IT, BUT...
...IT WOULD'VE BEEN NO SURPRISE IF I'D DIED THEN AND THERE TOO.

IF THAT'S ALL YOU'RE BASING IT ON, I CAN'T SAY I SEE IT YOUR WAY...
WHY NOT!?
'COS DATE-SAN'S BIMS ARE REMOTE CONTROL, REMEMBER?
ZA (ZSH)
ZA (ZSH)
DO (STOMP)
IF THEY WERE ANOTHER TYPE, THAT'D BE ONE THING.
BUT THOSE ARE RELATIVELY SAFE BIMS, IN THAT YOU CAN CALCULATE THE TIMING OF THEIR DETONATION, SEE?
DON'T YOU THINK MAYBE HE REALLY DID SAVE YOUR LIFE?
BTOOOM
Soldiers, be an

WHOA NOW, EASY THERE.
LAST TIME I ASK YOUR OPINION ON SOMETHING, RYOUTA!
WHATEVER!

SO... WHERE IS THIS STORE-ROOM?

THIS IS A PRETTY OLD BUILD-ING...

WE ARE STILL KEEPING HER LIVING HERE...
...A SECRET, RIGHT ...?
YOU BET.

DO YOU KNOW ?
NO! I FIGURED WE'D JUST ASK MURA-SAKI-SAN!

SHE DOESN'T KNOW WHERE IT IS ...?
THEN HOW DID SHE KNOW THERE EVEN WAS ONE TO START WITH ?

?

LOOKS LIKE SHE DOESN'T KNOW EXACTLY WHERE IT IS, SO...
...WE'LL JUST HAVE TO LOOK FOR IT.

UH-OH...

HUH ...? OH...
WELL ...

I HAVE AN AWFUL SENSE OF DIREC-TION...
OH YEAH... THAT'S RIGHT...

WHEN WE WERE HERE BEFORE... I GOT LOST...
...SO I DON'T REMEMBER WHERE IT WAS OR HOW I GOT THERE.

I SEE...
IN THAT CASE, WE SHOULD SPLIT UP TO FIND IT.

.....

ALL RIGHT.
I'LL TRY THE ANNEX.
I'LL CHECK OUT THE SECOND FLOOR.
IF YOU FIND IT, PLEASE LET US KNOW WITH A DOUBLE ECHO.

HERE I AM AGAIN...
IT HASN'T CHANGED A BIT IN THESE LAST SIX MONTHS.

PAK! (CRACK)
パキッ
PAK!
パキ

SIGN: MEDICAL STOREROOM

BUT NONE OF THAT MATTERS ...
DON (THUD)

I'LL JUST TOSS A FEW IN HERE TO MAKE IT LOOK LEGIT...

CAAAW!

ガア
CAW!
CAW! ガア
CAW! ガア

OH... DATE-SAN.

YOU FOUND IT ALREADY ...?

TH-THANK YOU SO MUCH.

GACHA (RATTLE)

BATAN (SHUT)

I FOUND SOME-THING THAT LOOKS LIKE AN ANTI-DOTE.

I ALSO PACKED SOME OTHER SUPPLIES I THOUGHT WE COULD USE, AS WELL AS GAUZE.

AND I'VE GOT BANDAGES AND ANTI-SEPTIC IN HERE.

YOU DON'T BY ANY CHANCE ...
...HAVE SUSPICIONS ABOUT ME, DO YOU?

HUH ...!?

SO...
I WANT TO TRUST YOU GUYS, AND I WANT TO BE TRUSTED BY YOU IN RETURN.
...NO MORE KEEPING SECRETS FROM ME, OKAY ...?

IF WE DON'T TRUST EACH OTHER HERE, WE'LL NEVER MAKE IT OUT ALIVE.

YES, I UNDER... STAND. SORRY.
HERE YOU GO...
I'LL LEAVE THIS TO YOU FOR THE TRIP BACK.
HUH ...? WHAT'S WITH THIS SENSE OF INTIMIDATION ...?
...SO PLEASE BE CAREFUL WITH IT.
I'VE PUT BOTTLES AND MEDICAL INSTRUMENTS IN THERE...

YOU TRUST PEOPLE TOO MUCH!
HUH ...!?
ピコレン
PIKOOOOON (PAAAANG)
OH... RIGHT.
BUT FIRST I'VE GOT TO CALL HIMIKO.
LET'S HURRY BACK NOW.

PHUNT STUNNING

...?

BA CLEAN

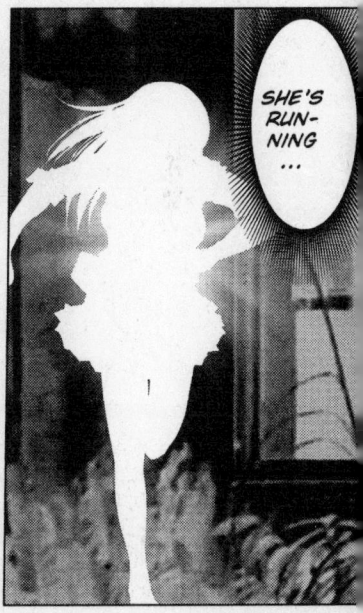
SHE'S RUN-NING ...

HFFA
HFFA
!!

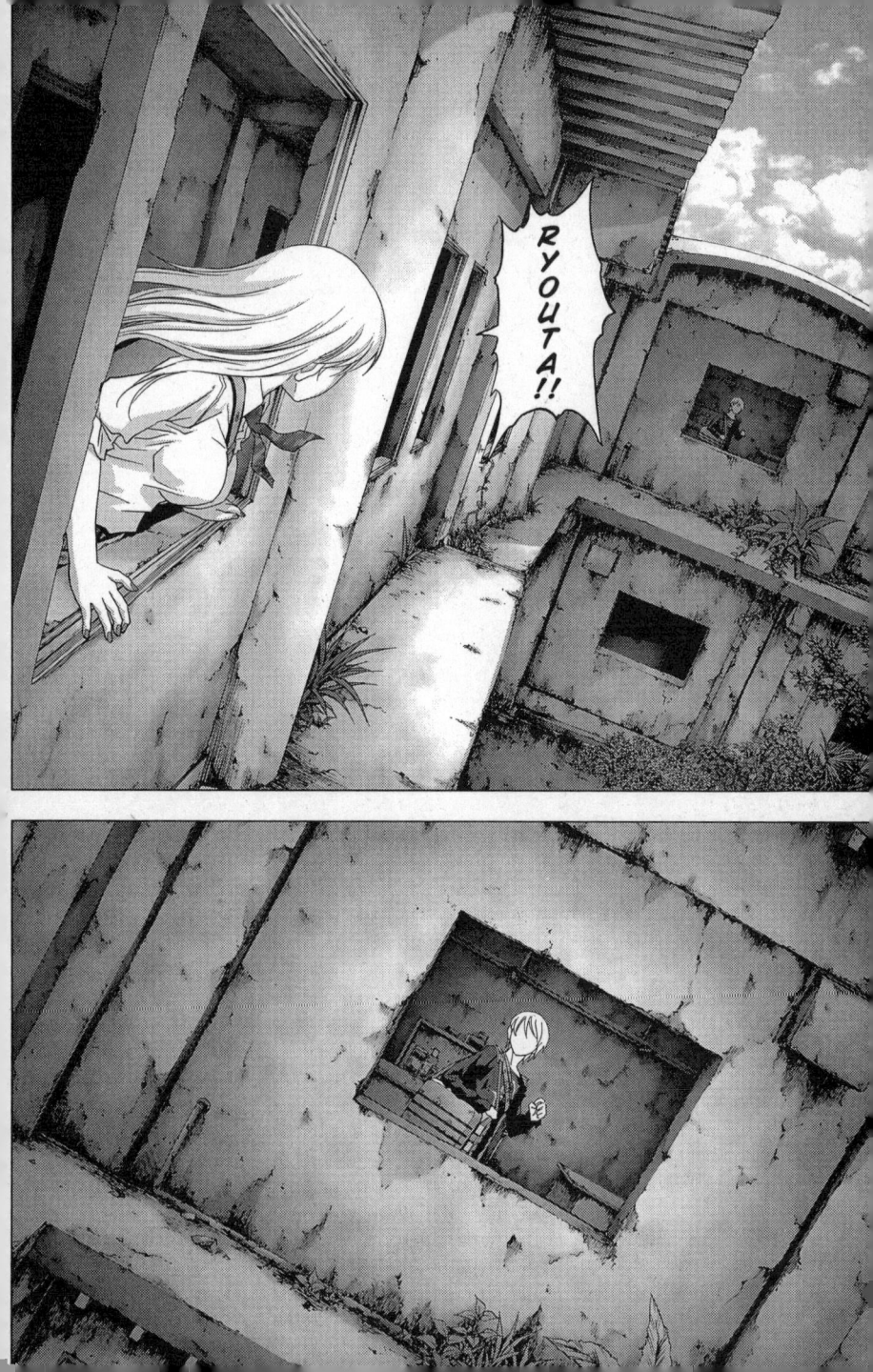
RYOUTA!!

WE FOUND THE MEDS!
YO, HIMIKO ...
LET'S GET BACK QUICK.

RYOUTA!!
DROP THAT CASE!!
THROW IT AWAY NOW!!

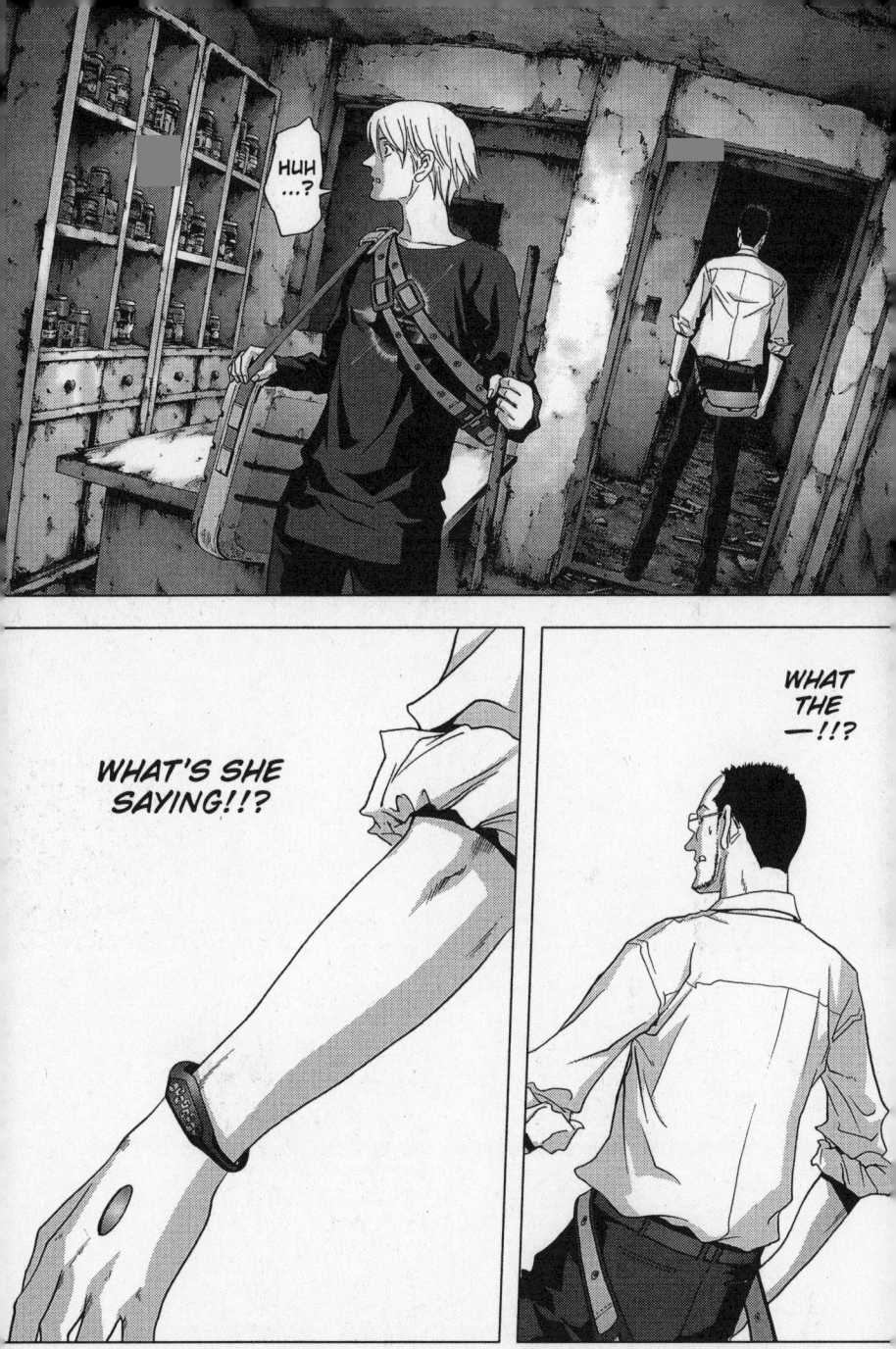
HUH ...?
WHAT'S SHE SAYING!!?
WHAT THE —!!?

.....
THERE'S A BOMB PLANTED IN THAT CAAASE —!!

WHAT!!?

BA
(WHIP)
THAT BITCH!!

DIE!!!
Pi

PiPiPi

DOGOUUUN
(KABOOOOOM)

BASA
BASA
BASA (FLAP)
GOOOOOO (RRRRRUMBLE)
GARAN (CRUMBLE)
GOOO (FWOOM)
BACHI
BACHI (CRICK)
BACHI

ゴゴゴ
GOOOO
……
KUH KUH KUH …
BWAH! HA! HA! HA! HA!
FIRST ONNE DOWN!!

RYOUTAA!!
RYOUTAA!!
NOOOO!!
AW, TOO BAD. YOUR BOY-FRIEND'S DEAD.
ZA (ZSH)
ZA
PACHI (CRACKLE)
PACHI
NOW I'M...
...ALL LOADED UP ON BIMS.
PACHI
PACHI
PACHI
PACHI

HOW'D YOU KNOW THERE WAS A BIM PLANTED IN THE CASE?

HEYY, LITTLE GIRL...

I-
I HAVE TO GET AWAY...
BUT...
RYOUTA'S DEAD...
...WHAT DO I DO AFTER...?

THE WEAK EXIST TO FEED THE STRONG.
THAT'S WHAT PROVIDENCE HAS IN STORE FOR THEM, NO MATTER WHAT.
I'M GONNA SURVIVE AND GO HOME AGAIN.
AND YOU'RE GONNA DIE TO GET ME THERE!!

YOU HAVEN'T CHANGED AT ALL...
...DATE-SENSEI...
THAT VOICE IS...?
TH—

DO
(SHNK)

SH-SHIKI ...!?
WHAT ARE YOU DOING, HIMIKO !!?
GET UP!!
RUN!!

45 Two Sacrifices

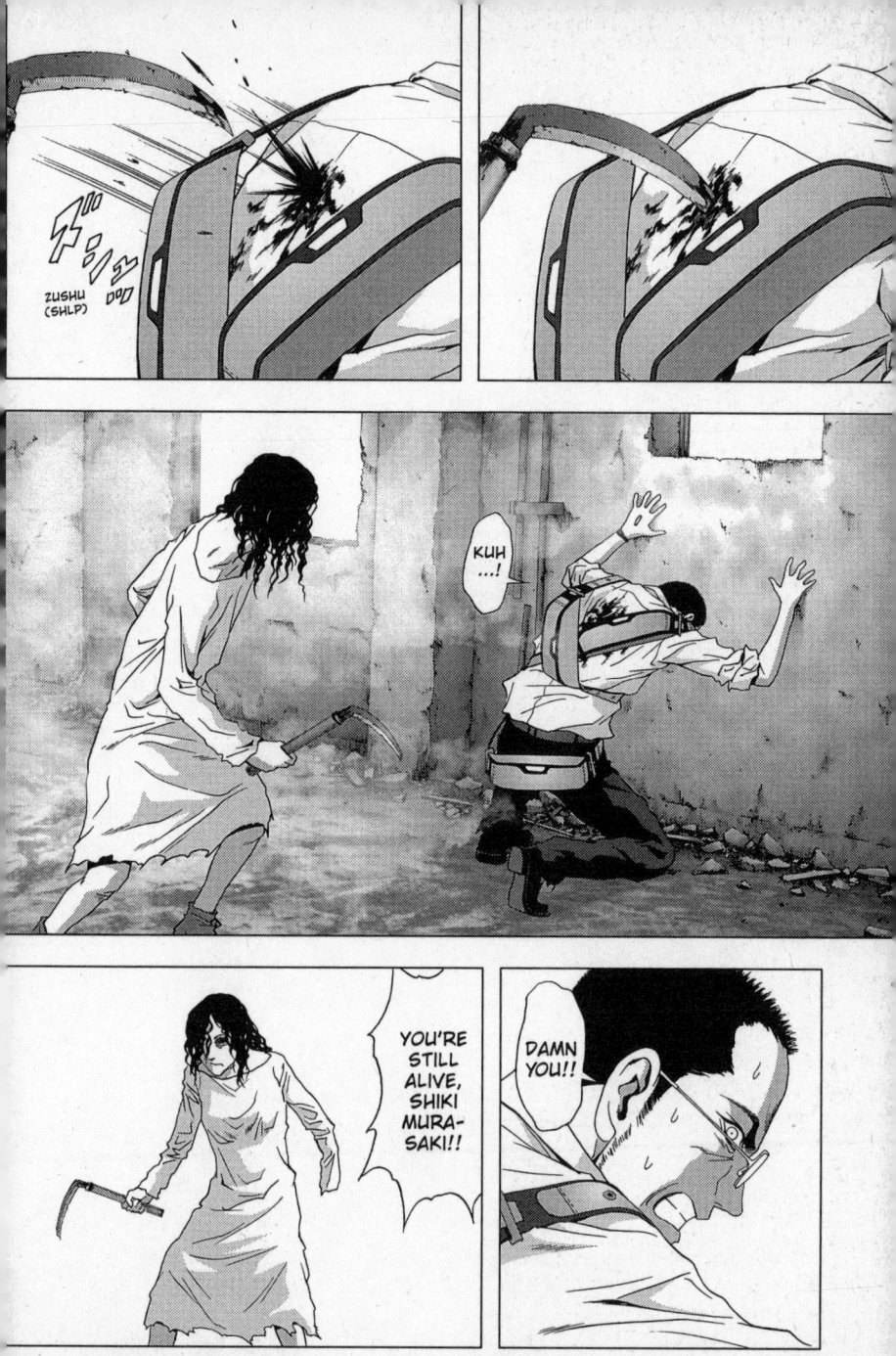
ZUSHU (SHLP)
KUH ...!
YOU'RE STILL ALIVE, SHIKI MURA-SAKI!!
DAMN YOU!!

THIRTY MINUTES EARLIER...
WHAT ARE YOU DOING, HIMIKO !!?
GET UP!! RUN!!
RYO...
RYOU-TA...
RYOU-TA'S...

ALL RIGHT.
I'LL TRY THE ANNEX.
I'LL CHECK OUT THE SECOND FLOOR.
IF YOU FIND IT, PLEASE LET US KNOW WITH A DOUBLE ECHO.
RYOUTA, WHY DON'T YOU COME WITH?
RIGHT!
OKAY, I'M GOING TO MURASAKI-SAN'S PLACE IN THE OTHER BUILDING TO ASK HER ABOUT THE STORE-ROOM.

OH...

WELL... I DON'T THINK SHE LIKES ME VERY MUCH, SO I'LL JUST STAY PUT.

O-OKAY...
...

BUT I STILL CAN'T SHAKE THE FEELING THAT DATE-SAN'S GONNA TRY TO KILL US.
RYOUTA, MAKE SURE YOU WATCH YOUR BACK.

WHAT?
NOTHING... IT'S JUST...

...YOU'VE STARTED CALLING ME BY MY FIRST NAME OUTTA THE BLUE, AND...
...I'M KINDA HAPPY ABOUT THAT...

SEE YA.
ANYWAY, I'LL BE CAREFUL.
OH NO, THAT WOULD BE BAAAD!
W-WELL, I COULD JUST BE...
HA HA HA ...
WHAT THE HECK !?
...PRETENDING TO LET MY GUARD DOWN, YOU KNOW?

AH ...! THIS MUST BE IT?
SIGN: MEDICAL STOREROOM
HUH...? DATE-SAN?
...SOMETHING FISHY ABOUT HIM...!!
THERE REALLY IS...
WHAT'S HE DOING HERE...?
HE WAS SUPPOSED TO BE CHECKING THE FIRST FLOOR...

THAT DOCTOR... YOU DEFINITELY CAN'T TRUST HIM.
I SEE...

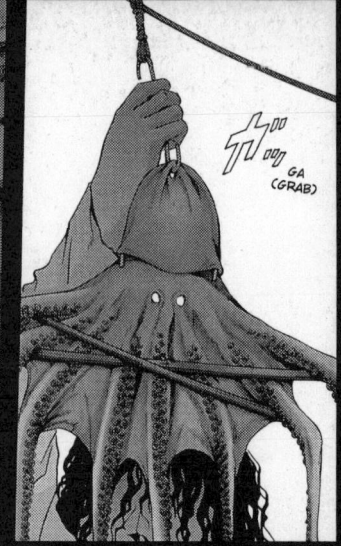
GA (GRAB)

SO COULD YOU JUST TELL ME WHERE THE MEDICAL STORE-ROOM IS?
I WON'T TELL HIM ABOUT YOU, MURA-SAKI-SAN.

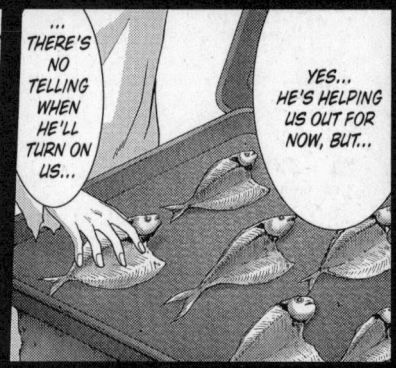
... THERE'S NO TELLING WHEN HE'LL TURN ON US...
YES... HE'S HELPING US OUT FOR NOW, BUT...

!
FOLLOW ME.
ZA (ZSH)
ZA

KASA (THUMP)

IT'S THE ROOM THROUGH THAT WINDOW.
YOU CAN SEE IT FROM HERE.
THAT'S DATE-SAN, THE DOCTOR I WAS TELLING YOU ABOUT.
OHHH, THAT GUY...
SOOO (SNEAK)
そぉぉ：
HIDE!!
BA (WHAP)
SOME-BODY'S THERE !!

WHAT DID YOU SAY !?
WH—
YOU!! JUST NOW ...!!
DID YOU SAY DATE !?
HUH ...?
YES...
SOOO (PEEK)
えっとぉ…

WHY'S HE BACK ON THE ISLAND?
THERE'S NO MISTAKE!!
UGH ...!
THAT'S DATE-SENSEI.
WHAT'S THE MATTER, MURASAKI-SAN?
MY LEFT ARM...
NEVER IMAGINED IT WOULD START ACHING AGAIN...

WHAAAT!?
THAT'S HIM.
THE MAN WHO DID THIS TO ME...
I CAN'T BELIEVE HE'S THE SAME GUY WHO PASSED OFF ALL THE BLAME TO MURASAKI-SAN FOR HIS OWN SCREWUP...
...AND EVEN AFTER HE GOT SENT TO THE ISLAND, TRICKED HER AGAIN...
...AND TOOK ALL THE CHIPS FOR HIMSELF TO MAKE HIS ESCAPE—

LIKE HOW HE KNOWS SO MUCH ABOUT THE GAME...
IF THAT'S THE CASE, IT ALL FITS.
...AND HIM TRYING TO KILL ME...

HUH ...? OH...
JUST THE REMOTE CONTROL TYPE.
I THINK HE MIGHT HAVE USED ONE OR TWO OF THEM...

WHAT KIND OF BIMS DOES HE HAVE NOW?

REMOTE CONTROL TYPE...

SO WHAT IS HE DOING THERE ALL BY HIM-SELF?
HE WAS SUPPOSED TO LET YOU KNOW WHEN HE'D FOUND THE STOREROOM, RIGHT?
THE ONLY PROBLEM IS FIGURING OUT WHEN.
LIS-TEN UP, OKAY ...?
HE'LL STAB YOU GUYS IN THE BACK FOR SURE.
I'VE GOT A BAD FEELING ABOUT THIS...
...HE'S BOOBY-TRAPPING THAT CASE WITH ONE OF HIS BIMS RIGHT NOW.
IT'S MORE THAN LIKELY THAT...

GOKU (GULP)
ゴクッ
RYOUTA DOESN'T SUSPECT DATE-SAN YET...
HERE COMES YOUR FRIEND.
NOT GOOD ...
BA (WHAP)
DON'T TAKE THAT CASE...
NO...

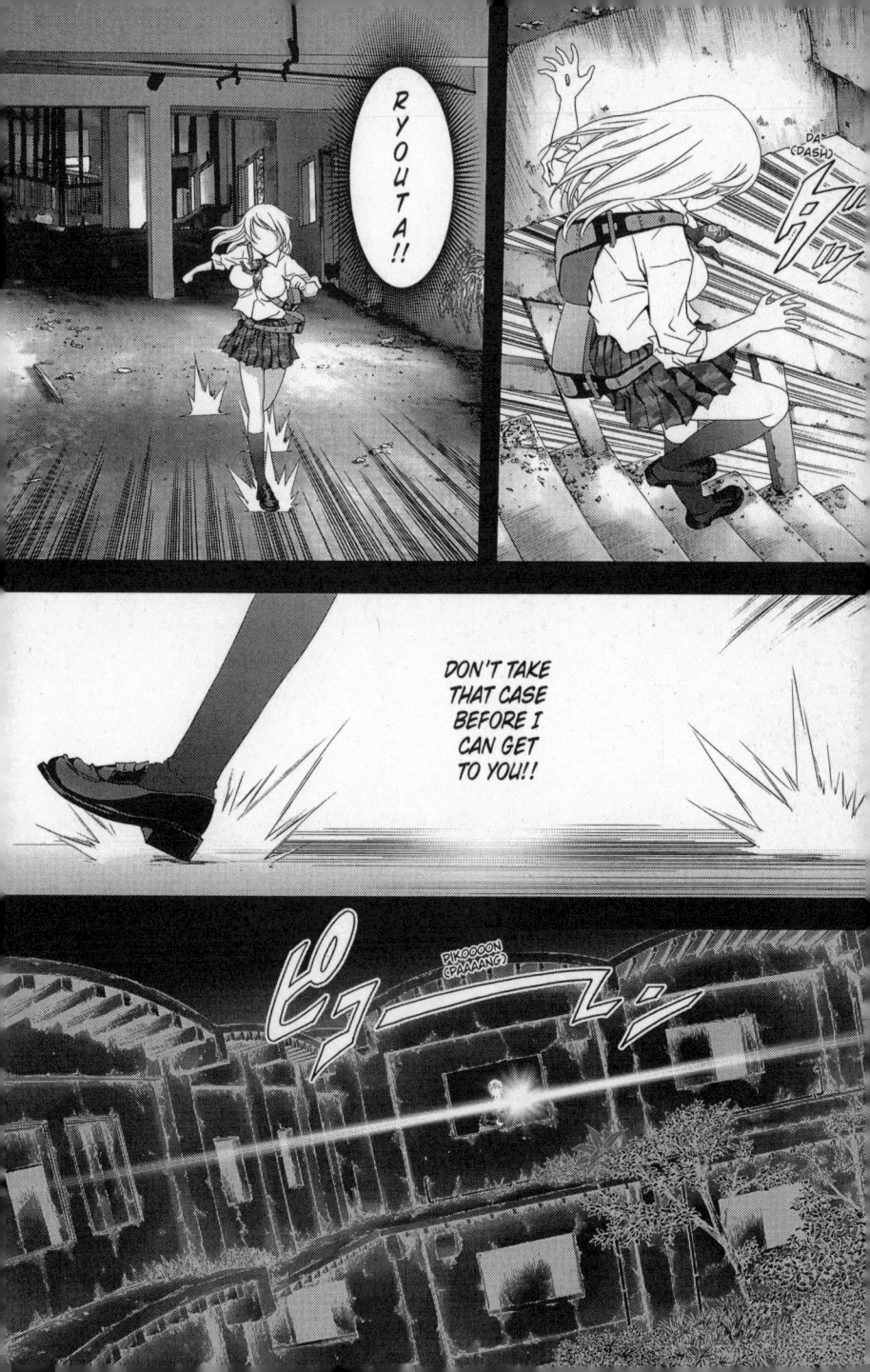
RYOUTA!!
DA-(DASH)
DON'T TAKE THAT CASE BEFORE I CAN GET TO YOU!!
PIKOOOON (PAAAANG)

JIJIJI (FREEZE)
PHIIIIN (PHIIING)
BA (POOP)
RYOUTA!!

!!
RYOUTA!!
DROP THAT CASE!!
THROW IT AWAY NOW!!
THERE'S A BOMB PLANTED IN THAT CAAASE —!!

Pi
AAH...

RYOUTAAAAAA!!
WE'RE RUN-NING FOR IT!!
PULL YOURSELF TOGETH-ER!!

I'VE ALREADY LAID MY BIMS.

IT'S NO USE RUN-NING.

POGOUUUN (KABOOOM)

NUM-BER SIX!!
Pi

ARE YOU OKAY, HIMIKO!?
KOFF!
KOFF!
PARA (CRUMBLE)
パラ
PARA
パラ
KOFF!
KOFF!
HRK!
THESE HALLWAYS ARE TOO DANGER-OUS!!
IF HIMIKO HADN'T STUMBLED, WE'D BOTH BE DEAD RIGHT NOW!!
HE'S LAID TRAPS WITH HIS BIMS ...!!
WE'LL BE SAFER ON THE ROOF!!
WE'RE GOING OUT THIS WAY.

TOOK CARE OF THAT BLOWN-UP ARM YOUR-SELF, HUH?

BRAVO, BRAVO...

THAT TAKES BALLS.

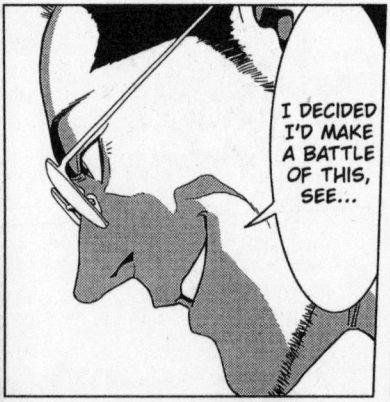
I DECIDED I'D MAKE A BATTLE OF THIS, SEE...

YOU'VE ALREADY SET YOUR REMOTE TYPES THROUGH-OUT THE BUILDING, HAVEN'T YOU?
YOU...

IF YOU WANNA GET OUT, YOU'LL HAVE TO KILL ME OFF FOR GOOD THIS TIME.
I'VE LAID OUT ALL MY BIMS TO COMPLETELY ISOLATE THIS AREA.
I KNOW WHERE EACH AND EVERY NUMBER IS.

POOR THING'S ALL MIXED UP INSIDE, AND SHE DOESN'T KNOW WHAT TO DO, HMM?
SHE JUST SAW HER BOY-FRIEND DIE.
CAN'T BLAME HER.
THE LITTLE GIRL'S LOST HER WILL TO FIGHT, HASN'T SHE?

I'LL KILL YOU WITH YOUR BOY'S BIMS.
YOU WON'T BE FAR BEHIND HIM.
DON'T YOU FRET, MY DEAR.
I'VE GOT THIS, SO YOU GO HIDE.
NOT ON MY WATCH !!
BA (WHAP)
BUN (HURL)

KA
(CLACK)
WHAT THE —!?

DOGOUUUU (KABOOOOM)
YOU GOT TOO COCKY.
IF SHE HITS THE SWITCH FOR ME, I CAN FIGHT TOO.
IT'S TWO TO ONE.
NOW WHO'S SCREWED?
Pi
GOOOO (FWOOOM)
GUH!
ZU (SKSH)

I NEVER FOR A MOMENT FORGOT YOU OR WHAT YOU DID.
I WON'T FOR-GIVE YOU ...
TA
TA (TMP)
TA
AND I CURSED THE PERSON I WAS THEN.
THE MORON ...
THE NAIVE LITTLE IDIOT ...
...DON'T YOU THINK IT'S AN ACT OF GOD!?
GET-TING TO MEET YOU AGAIN LIKE THIS...
I WAS A FOOL ...
I HAD TOO MUCH FAITH IN LOVE.

DA (DASH)
ST-STAY AWAY FROM MEEE!!
ZA (ZSH)
HOLD IT!!
YOU REALLY THOUGHT YOU COULD CORNER ME JUST LIKE THAT?
JUST GOES TO SHOW THAT THE WEAK...
...WILL NEVER BE ANY-THING MORE THAN WEAK...
Pi

EH ...!? THAT CAME FROM THE OTHER SIDE OF THE WALL...
PiPi
(GAAAAN (BOOOOOM)

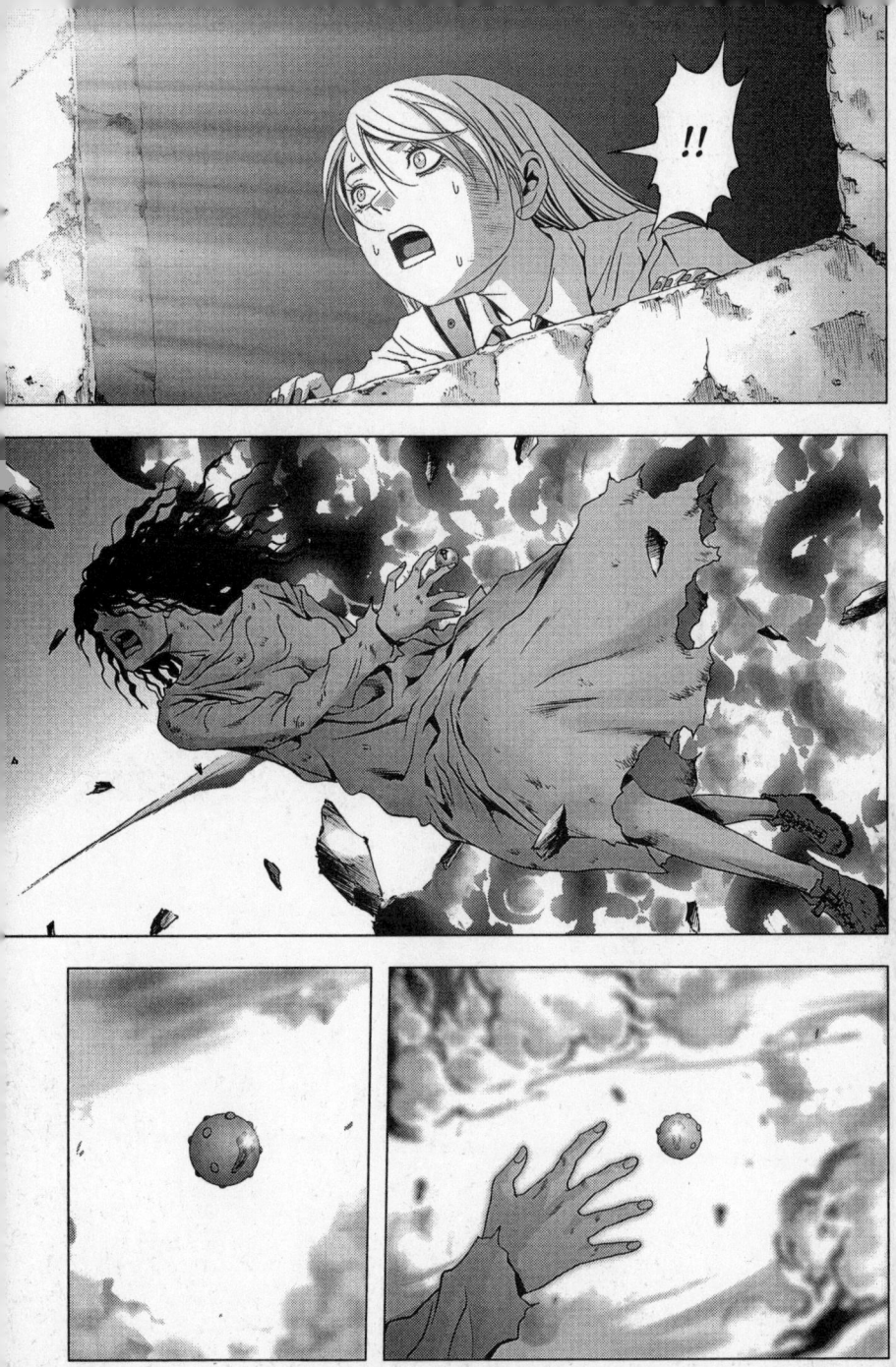

DOGOUUUUUN
(KABOOOOM)
GARA
GARA
(CRUMBLE)
GARA
NOOOO!!

WHOA!!
GOOOO (ROOOOAR)
GARA
GARA
GARA

THAT'S WHAT YOU GET.
YOU SHOULDA JUST LAID DOWN AND DIED, NICE AND QUIET...

GOGOOOON (RUMBLE)
THE WHOLE DAMN BUILDING'S COMING DOWN ...
THAT WAS CLOSE ...

THIS'LL BE A PIECE OF CAKE.
AND THEN I'LL HAVE TWO CHIPS... KUH KUH KUH.

NOW... ONLY ONE LEFT IS THE GIRL, AND SHE'S ALREADY GIVEN UP.

RYOUTA !!
MURA-SAKI-SAN!!
I- I NEED A BIM ...
HE'S COMING.
I CAN'T SIT HERE CRYING NOW.
I CAN'T THINK STRAIGHT.
I-IT'S NO USE...

OHH YEAH...
I- I'LL JUST HAVE TO RUN...
I ALMOST FORGOT.
THIS WHOLE PLACE IS LACED WITH BIMS...

GAME OVER
...I'M GONNA DIE,
AND JUST LIKE THAT...
...AND DECIDED I WANTED TO LIVE...
AFTER I TRIED SO HARD...

...WOULD HIT ME THIS HARD—
I NEVER IMAGINED RYOUTA'S DEATH...
EVEN BEFORE ALL THIS, HE WAS ALWAYS BY MY SIDE.
...HE WAS SO POSITIVE AND ENCOUR-AGING.
WHEN I COULDN'T STAND REALITY AND RAN AWAY TO THE VIRTUAL WORLD...
...IT'D END LIKE THIS...
I-IF I'D KNOWN...

I WISH I'D TOLD HIM THE TRUTH!!
...I WOULD'VE TOLD HIM I WAS HIMIKO.
IT'S ALL OVER FOR YOU NOW.
BUT LET ME ASK YOU ONE LAST THING.

WHY DON'T YOU JOIN ME?
IF WE TEAM UP, WE'LL GET THE CHIPS WE NEED TO GET OFF THIS ISLAND IN NO TIME.
WE'LL GET OUT ALIVE. TRUST ME, I KNOW WHAT I'M TALKING ABOUT.
HOW ABOUT IT? NOT A BAD PROPO-SITION, RIGHT?
LIAR!!
THAT'S WHAT YOU SAID TO MURA-SAKI-SAN!!

I SEE...
SO YOU ALREADY KNOW...
FINE THEN, DIE.
KACHI (CLICK)
カチ

I'M OKAY WITH THIS...
WHEN IT'S TIME...

WHEN IT'S TIME TO DIE...
BA (WHIP)

...I'LL DO IT WITH DIGNITY AND GRACE ...

GOOD-BYE...
...MAMA!!
BO (BOOMF)

YON
(BOUNCE)

KORO (ROLL)
コロ
KORO
コロ
KON (KONK)
コン
KACHI
KACHI
THE DETONATION SWITCH WON'T ENGAGE !?
KACHI (CLICK)
KACHI
KACHI
WHY DIDN'T IT GO OFF!?
WHAT THE HELL !?
DOES THAT MEAN OWNERSHIP HASN'T TRANSFERRED TO ME!?

PUUN (SHIING)
WHICH MEANS...
PIKOOOON (PAAAANG)
SI (FIZZAR)
...HE'S...
SI
SI
...STILL ALIVE!?
TO BE CONTINUED IN BTOOOM! 8

MRAC
05/15

BTOOOM! 7

JUNYA INOUE

Translation: Christine Dashiell • Lettering: Terri Delgado

This book is a work of fiction. Names, characters, places, and incidents are the product of the author's imagination or are used fictitiously. Any resemblance to actual events, locales, or persons, living or dead, is coincidental.

BTOOOM! © Junya INOUE 2009. All rights reserved. English translation rights arranged with SHINCHOSHA PUBLISHING CO. through Tuttle-Mori Agency, Inc., Tokyo.

English translation © 2014 by Hachette Book Group, Inc.

All rights reserved. In accordance with the U.S. Copyright Act of 1976, the scanning, uploading, and electronic sharing of any part of this book without the permission of the publisher is unlawful piracy and theft of the author's intellectual property. If you would like to use material from the book (other than for review purposes), prior written permission must be obtained by contacting the publisher at permissions@hbgusa.com. Thank you for your support of the author's rights.

Yen Press
Hachette Book Group
237 Park Avenue, New York, NY 10017

www.HachetteBookGroup.com
www.YenPress.com

Yen Press is an imprint of Hachette Book Group, Inc. The Yen Press name and logo are trademarks of Hachette Book Group, Inc.

First Yen Press Edition: August 2014

ISBN: 978-0-316-24544-9

10 9 8 7 6 5 4 3 2 1

BVG

Printed in the United States of America

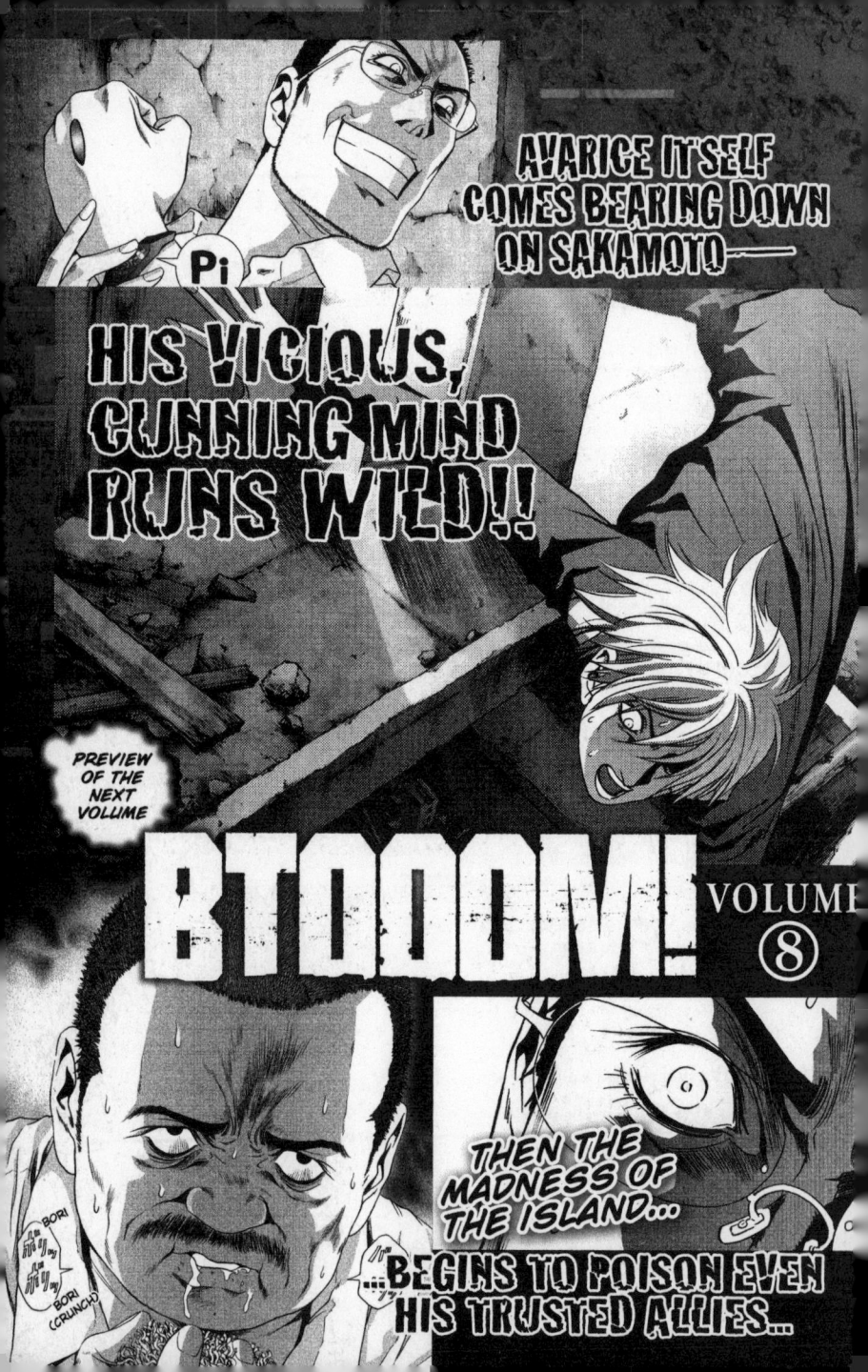
Pi
AVARICE IT'SELF COMES BEARING DOWN ON SAKAMOTO——
HIS VICIOUS, CUNNING MIND RUNS WILD!!
PREVIEW OF THE NEXT VOLUME
BTOOOM! VOLUME 8
BORI
BORI (CRUNCH)
THEN THE MADNESS OF THE ISLAND...
...BEGINS TO POISON EVEN HIS TRUSTED ALLIES...